WANTED FOR MURDER

Robert P. "Bobby" Nauss. Warlock. Former biker. Implicated in t' █████████ f █████ ████ young women in the █████

WANTED F █

Theresa Mari█ ███████████████ artist. Convicted fo ████████████████ rman. Escaped and apprehended three times. Her fourth escape proved successful.

WANTED FOR MURDER

Leo Joseph Koury. Businessman owner of gay bars. And killer of competition. Has successfully evaded capture so long that he no longer can be prosecuted for many of his crimes.

WANTED FOR MURDER

Killers from coast to coast, in the North and in the South, and in the files of local police and the FBI, who continue to hunt for the deadly criminals who threaten all of us.

WANTED FOR MURDER

True crime at its most gripping, and the latest triumph of the authors of *The Only Living Witness*, praised by Mary Higgins Clark as "an instant classic . . . goes beyond *In Cold Blood* in depicting the relentless horror of cold-blooded murder."

With a forceful introduction by Vernon J. Geberth, former commanding officer of The Bronx Area Detective Task Force of the New York Police Department.

WANTED FOR MURDER

Stephen G. Michaud
and
Hugh Aynesworth

A SIGNET BOOK

SIGNET
Published by the Penguin Group
Penguin Books USA Inc., 375 Hudson Street,
New York, New York 10014, U.S.A.
Penguin Books Ltd, 27 Wrights Lane,
London W8 5TZ, England
Penguin Books Australia Ltd, Ringwood,
Victoria, Australia
Penguin Books Canada Ltd, 2801 John Street,
Markham, Ontario, Canada L3R 1B4
Penguin Books (N.Z.) Ltd, 182-190 Wairau Road,
Auckland 10, New Zealand

Penguin Books Ltd, Registered Offices:
Harmondsworth, Middlesex, England

First published by Signet, an imprint of New American
Library, a division of Penguin Books USA Inc.

First Printing, October, 1990
10 9 8 7 6 5 4 3 2 1

CONTENTS

INTRODUCTION

It is my privilege to offer this introduction to *Wanted for Murder,* Stephen G. Michaud and Hugh Aynesworth's unique collection of murder vignettes. These stories reach well beyond impersonal homicide statistics to capture the personal aspects of each case. Michaud and Aynesworth provide the reader with an insider's view of homicide, a look at murder from the homicide detective's perspective.

As a homicide detective, consultant, and police instructor on the subject of violent-death investigation, I have worked with more than 300 federal, state and local law enforcement agencies in the course of investigating, researching and assessing approximately 5,000 homicides throughout the United States. Out of this experience, I can attest to the fact that popular crime literature, fact or fiction, usually focuses on the intricate, complex or sensational cases that may shock or amaze a civilian audience, but that account for only a tiny fraction of a typical homicide detective's caseload.

Outrageous and puzzling cases such as Green

River and the other serial killers discussed at the end of *Wanted for Murder* are an undeniable problem for law enforcement, because of the inherent difficulty of stopping these seemingly motiveless murderers, and because their depredations are costly and time-consuming to investigate. But day-to-day, the real world of homicide is more exactly captured in cases such as that of the arsonist Vásquez brothers in El Paso, Texas (page 43), or wife killer William Smith of Minnetonka, Minnesota (page 107), entirely different individuals who nevertheless are alike in the one way that matters to a homicide investigator: They are murderers.

Nor does *Wanted for Murder* lack for the bizarre and mysterious episodes that also are part of the homicide detective's routine. These include the curious tale of Lyons, Nebraska, police chief Gregory Jon Webb, wanted for the murder of his downstairs neighbor; William Fischer of Southampton, New York, apparently responsible for the murder of his own son as well as his boy's female companion; and Rick Church of Woodstock, Illinois, who appears to have assaulted his former girlfriend's father with a trash stick.

The motives behind many of the killings are both trivial and tragic. Familiar to any cop are the wife and girlfriend murderers who, out of jealousy or twisted macho logic, perpetrate violence on women and then explain why: "If I can't have her, no one can."

Most of these characters probably would not have committed their crimes without the artificial courage they find in liquor bottles, vials and syringes. Still another class of criminal kills for money; either as thieves or, as is now common in American urban areas, as "hitmen" for other felons, such as drug smugglers and distributors. Also, there are killers who slay only to cover up other crimes. Robert Chickene, the Missoula, Montana, biker (page 35), is an example of this subspecies.

The killers in this book contribute to the growing violence of American society and create the daily carnage that confronts homicide investigators. As a professional, I see it as my duty to act as an advocate for the victims of these killers as well as for their survivors. All cops, I believe, and especially homicide detectives, have a profound responsibility in this regard. I feel this very strongly. As long as any of the psychopaths, social dropouts, psychotic personalities and other killers in *Wanted for Murder* remain at large, a heinous crime remains unpunished and our so-called justice system has suffered another failure.

Wanted for Murder could help right those wrongs. Readers who recognize these fugitives can notify the appropriate authorities and, in most cases, earn a reward if the killer is caught. I sincerely hope they do.

May justice prevail.

—Vernon J. Geberth

Note: Vernon Geberth is a retired homicide commander with the New York City Police Department and author of the standard textbook *Practical Homicide Investigation: Tactics, Procedures and Forensic Techniques.* He is a nationally renowned authority on the subject of violent and sudden death. Geberth is currently president of PHI Investigative Consultants, Inc., in New York State.

AUTHORS' NOTE

With the single exception of Edward Edgar Nye, who is included in these pages at the request of the New York State Police, all thirty-eight of our profiled fugitives have been convicted of murder, charged with murder or are suspects wanted for questioning in connection with open murder investigations. As best can be determined, all were at large in the first week of May 1990.

As a group, the thirty-four male and four female fugitives are implicated in the slayings of thirty-three male and nineteen female victims. The killers' weapons ranged from a hangman's noose to a cloth gag soaked in toxic carbon tetrachloride. The most popular method of murder by far, however, was by firearm. Thirty-four victims were shot. Seven others were stabbed. Six died in a fire, two were bludgeoned, one was poisoned, one was suffocated, and another apparently died of a broken neck.

The youngest killer at the time of the crime was William Leslie Arnold, who had not yet turned seventeen when he shot his parents in

September 1959. Arnold has also been on the lam the longest, twenty-three years since he escaped from a Nebraska prison. The youngest victim was sixteen-month-old Jessie Ganote.

The oldest killer overall—as well as at the time of his crime—is William Smith, who was born in 1924 and was fifty-two years old when he allegedly shot his ex-wife Joan in a Minnetonka, Minnesota, motel room in 1977. The oldest victim was seventy-two-year-old Rafael Gonzalez, who perished in the El Paso apartment-house blaze allegedly set by the Vasquez brothers.

Twenty-six, or exactly half, of the victims knew their slayers, or were related to them. Fourteen were murdered by complete strangers. In the balance of the cases, it is impossible to determine whether or not victim and killer were acquainted prior to the murder.

Twenty-three of the killers were of Anglo-European backgrounds. Seven were Hispanic and seven others were blacks. One fugitive, Leo Koury, is of Lebanese descent. Thirty-three victims were Anglo-European. Seven were black and twelve were Hispanic. Three killings were interracial.

In all, at least $58,000 has been offered in reward money, $25,000 for Leo Koury alone. However, because the amount of the potential reward in many cases is unspecified, the overall recapture value of the thirty-eight fugitives probably comfortably exceeds $100,000.

Among the dead were five law enforcement officers. Among the fugitives is one former police chief.

Our primary means of identifying fugitives to

profile was through local, state, and federal law enforcement agencies. We explained our criteria to each and encouraged all to offer their toughest or most egregious cases. Some organizations, such as the Massachusetts Department of Correction, and the New York State Police, operate dedicated and extremely successful fugitive-apprehension programs. These law enforcement groups eagerly accepted the opportunity to place their most-wanted felons in this book.

Other state and local jurisdictions—some notable by their absence from these pages—out of indifference or indolence, couldn't be bothered to participate or were too poorly organized to take advantage of the oppurtunity. In one instance, an agency candidly explained its problems in a letter to us. In the note, a press-relations officer related that her department once maintained a most-wanted list from which we formerly might have chosen a candidate felon.

However, she continued, "there seems to be a lot of movement to and from the lists. Recently, we had a case of a felon who had been sought for a murder from several years ago and he was in fact on the list. He was finally taken into custody and brought into court for a preliminary hearing. Unfortunately, some of the witnesses had moved or died and the ones we were able to contact had a sudden case of memory lapse. The state's attorney had to release the individual due to insufficient evidence to prosecute the individual.

"At any rate, our chief of detectives feels that it is too difficult to provide anyone with a current list of wanted criminals. Under the circumstances, we regret we cannot participate in your project."

We regretted it, too. However, *Wanted for Murder* is the first in a projected series of books that will report on unsolved murder cases as well as other areas of police work beyond fugitive hunting. We would like to encourage all law enforcement agencies to consider sharing this type of information with us, under the usual protocols. Any police organization wishing to contact us in this regard may do so, on official agency stationery only, at the address listed below.

WANTED FOR MURDER©
PO BOX 59026
DALLAS, TEXAS 75229-1026
FAX: (214) 358-0100

SECTION ONE

WEST AND SOUTHWEST

1. His Brother's Widow

MICHAEL DEAN CLARKE
Renton, Washington

DATE OF BIRTH: DECEMBER 2, 1951
HEIGHT: FIVE FEET, NINE INCHES
WEIGHT: 170 POUNDS
HAIR: BLOND
EYES: BLUE
OTHER: MAY SEEK WORK AS A REFRIGERATION MECHANIC
REWARD: NONE
CONTACT: DETECTIVE EARL TRIPP
         KING COUNTY DEPARTMENT OF PUBLIC SAFETY
         (206) 296-7530

The only significant character flaw that Peggy Teeters, née Holder, ever saw in her younger sister Gail was her lack of assertiveness and independent spirit. "I thought Gail needed to grow, expand, be on her own," says Peggy. But Gail didn't get the chance to act on Peggy's advice. Instead, she was murdered. Her big sister explains how it happened.

The Holder girls, Peggy, Gail and Paula, all were raised in Renton, a small town in rainy western Washington, just east of Seattle. Peggy remembers that early in junior high school—at age thirteen—Gail met her first real boyfriend, Allan Clarke. She never dated anyone else. Al-

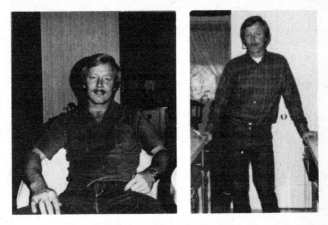

Michael Dean Clarke
(Photo Courtesy Peggy Teeters)

lan and Gail were married in 1978, before her twentieth birthday. In 1982 Gail bore Allan a daughter, Shyla Kay.

Just three years later, in July of 1985, Allan Clarke died of a brain aneurysm. Gail suddenly was widowed, a young mother with little education, no particular skills and scant experience of the world outside her family. The first thing she did after Allan died was move in with Peggy and her husband, Gary Teeters. Peggy and Gary had two children, a daughter named Mandi and a son, Jake.

Peggy thought that her grieving sister needed to avoid another dependent relationship. As Ms. Teeters says, she felt it was time for Gail to expand and grow. Yet only three months after Allan's funeral, Gail started seeing someone new, her deceased husband's older brother, Michael Dean Clarke, then thirty-three. It was not long afterward that the trouble began.

Mike Clarke had a ferocious temper, easily provoked when he drank, which he did often and to excess. His ex-wife, Shirley, was once forced to obtain a restraining order against him, swearing in her affidavit to the court that Clarke "was threatening, abusive and physically violent toward me." Peggy Teeters recalls learning from Gail that Mike on one occasion had broken Shirley's arm.

In 1982, Shirley Clarke divorced Mike. The same year he robbed a Renton clothing store and was caught, convicted and sent to prison. He was released in March of 1985 and returned to Renton, where he enrolled in a refrigeration-mechanics class and worked for his mother, who paid her son to do handyman jobs around the ceramics shop she owned. One condition of his parole was that Clarke undergo counseling for his alcoholism. He did, and for a while it seemed that Mike Clarke finally was going to straighten out his life.

"Gail," says Peggy, "told me that Mike was nice as he could be when he wasn't drinking." But soon enough Mike was drinking— occasionally—and then regularly, and then he started abusing Gail. "She told me he'd hit her, knock her around and stuff," Peggy recalls. It soon got so bad that Gail and Shyla Kay, who had been renting a trailer from Mike Clarke's parents (Shyla Kay's grandparents), moved back in with the Teeters for a time.

Then Mike swore he'd reform and she gave

him another chance. Their relationship lasted until early February of 1986 when Gail again asked if she and her daughter could move in with the Teeters. Gail would not tell her sister and brother-in-law exactly what had happened, "but she was so afraid of him," says Peggy, "that she would not go back to the trailer alone to get her stuff. She was afraid he'd be there."

Gail Clarke told Mike to get out of her life on Saturday, February 8, 1986. The next Friday—Valentine's Day—he drove to the Teeters' house to announce personally that he was leaving town for Montana, where he had friends and relatives. Peggy was at home for Mike's bitter farewell that day and she felt his implacable enmity toward her. Mike knew Peggy had been urging her sister Gail to break away from him. "When he left that night, he looked right at me," explains Peggy. "And he said I would be sorry. He didn't say Gail would be sorry. He said, 'You'll be sorry,' and was looking right at me."

Three days later, on the afternoon of Monday the seventeenth, Gail drove her daughter Shyla Kay over to her Aunt Kay's (Allan and Mike's sister) house where Shyla Kay was to spend the night. Then Gail picked up Peggy at the Toys R Us outlet where Ms. Teeters worked, and drove her sister home. They cooked and ate dinner at the Teeterses' and then washed the dishes together before settling in to watch television.

"We were sitting there watching TV," Peggy says, "and Gail mentioned that this was the first time since Allan died that she'd been totally alone in the house. My daughter Mandi heard and said she'd spend the night with her, which was fine with me. So Mandi gathered up her school things and away they went."

Mandi would be the sole witness to the few hours that Gail Clarke had left.

The little girl, then nine, recalls watching television with Aunt Gail at the trailer. Then Uncle Mike, who was supposed to be in Montana, knocked at the door. Her aunt sent Mandi Teeters back to her bed and told her niece she'd been in to cuddle up with her in a while. Gail did return to her bedroom, and apparently felt no fear. She hugged Mandi and told her good night. Soon, both females were dozing soundly together.

Sometime later in the night, a bloodcurdling scream from her aunt, "Mandi! Mandi!" tore Mandi Teeters into startled wakefulness. She could tell someone was on the bed with them. It was Uncle Mike. He had a knife and was plunging it into Gail. But Mandi only registered her aunt's screams in the darkness. "Daddy! Daddy!" she called for her father. And then "Mandi!" again.

Uncle Mike ordered Mandi out of the bed and into Shyla Kay's room across the hall. She obeyed in a daze. Later—she doesn't know how long—he came into Shyla's room and began to stab Mandi, superficially, with the knife. He cut her seven times, apparently taking sadistic delight in torturing the girl.

As Mandi Teeters tells the story, she then broke away and ran into Aunt Gail's room, seeing for the first time what Mike Clarke had come to do with his knife. She also saw a stick on the floor and grabbed it up for protection.

But Uncle Mike came after her and took the stick and beat the girl with it.

He may have thought he'd killed her. As best the doctors and Mandi's mother can tell, the girl lapsed into a limp state of semiconsciousness from the stabbing and beating. She'd later be able to recall Uncle Mike showering and changing his clothes and riffling through Aunt Gail's purse. She would also remember looking at the bedside clock once and noting the time was twelve. But the bedroom curtains were all drawn and Mandi couldn't tell if it was midnight or noon.

The next morning, Tuesday the eighteenth, Gail Clarke was to have driven her niece to school. When Mandi did not show up, the attendance office (which was aware that Peggy Teeters worked and that her sisters helped transport her children to and from school) telephoned Paula Clarke. She told the school to call Gail. When Gail Clarke's phone didn't answer, the attendance office gave up. No one dialed Peggy at work. Not until five o'clock that day did it dawn on Paula and Peggy and the rest of the family that Gail was missing and that no one had seen her or Peggy's daughter since Monday night.

Paula and her husband Bart sped to the trailer and were there trying to jimmy the door lock when Gary Teeters pulled up. In a panic of fear for Gail and his daughter, Teeters smashed his fist through the glass door and opened it into the darkened trailer. Paula, who knew the interior layout by heart, rushed past him inside and felt her way back to her sister's bedroom. The next thing Gary and Bart heard was her scream as she flicked on the overhead light and was confronted with the horrifying tableau; Gail Clarke dead and covered with blood in her bed with little Mandi lying there too, bloodied and barely conscious.

On Wednesday, February 19, Mike Clarke was formally charged with Gail Clarke's murder and the attempted murder of Mandi Teeters. He was already long gone, with at least a twelve-hour head start on the police in his 1977 red Fiat Spider. Peggy Teeters reports that the car was recovered in Oregon. There are no other clues to his whereabouts.

Mandi Teeters mended completely from her physical injuries. But her parents, who are now also raising Shyla Kay Clarke, are mindful of the fact that Mandi was an eyewitness and of what Mike Clarke said to Peggy the last time she saw him. Gary and Peggy will not rest until Clarke is permanently behind bars. Understandably, Gary and Peggy have been very fearful, and highly protective of Mandi.

But the good news is that Shyla Kay's cousin has refused to crumble under the psychological trauma she suffered that harrowing night in the trailer. Mandi has responded well to psychological counseling. "Her doctor," says Peggy Teeters, "can't believe how well Mandi has adjusted, how strong-willed she is. She always tells me that when boys pick on her at school, she slams 'em up against the wall and says, 'Nobody will ever hit me again.' She's very tough."

2. "I Shot the Cop"

ENRIQUE MORENO CASAS
Fort Worth, Texas

DATE OF BIRTH: MARCH 6, 1967
HEIGHT: FIVE FEET, SEVEN INCHES
WEIGHT: 160 POUNDS
HAIR: BLACK, USUALLY WORN SHORT
EYES: BROWN
DISTINGUISHING MARKS OR SCARS: "RICKY" TATTOOED ON ONE LEG; A LIKENESS OF THE VIRGIN MARY TATTOOED ON UPPER LEFT ARM; A GRIM REAPER TATTOOED ON UPPER RIGHT ARM
ALSO KNOWN AS: "RICKY" OR "HENRY"
REWARD: $5,000
CONTACT: FORT WORTH POLICE DEPARTMENT
SERGEANT H.L. WYATT
(817) 877-8282

At the time of his murder in 1986, tall, thick-shouldered deputy Frank Howell, thirty-eight, was a popular and respected veteran member of the Tarrant County, Texas, Sheriff's Department. His acts of kindness and bravery were well known to local cops. Once, at the scene of a reported domestic disturbance, Howell found instead a destitute mother with her hungry children. He gave the woman twenty-five dollars to feed her family. Another time, the officer risked

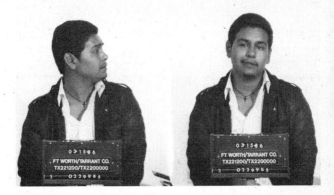

Enrique Moreno Casas

his own life to save that of an elderly woman trapped in her burning house. According to Frank Howell's family preacher, the Baptist Reverend Dennis Swanberg, he was "a gentle giant who had a tough skin but a very tender heart."

Enrique Casas, a native of Mexico, was just nineteen, half Frank Howell's age, the night Casas allegedly murdered the deputy. Enrique was a member of the so-called Vario gang of south Fort Worth—"a loose-knit bunch of punks," says detective Gaylin Cook of the Fort Worth police's fugitive unit. Casas had been arrested twice in 1986—in March for possession of marijuana and in September for attempted burglary.

The cop and his killer met in the early evening of November 3, 1986. Officer Howell, at the wheel of an unmarked car, noticed Casas and a friend, sixteen-year-old Sammy Flores, in Cas-as's vehicle, a brown Chevy Monte Carlo, parked behind an American Legion post in far south Fort Worth. Howell at that moment had with him an arrest warrant for an Hispanic male who also drove a brown Monte Carlo. That is why he pulled his cream-colored county car into the lot.

As Sammy Flores later told the story in his statement to the police, he and Casas had stopped in the parking lot to check the Monte Carlo's oil. When Officer Howell pulled up, Sammy said, he was in the car and Casas was standing outside. Howell asked to see Casas's driver's license, and then inquired if Casas was carrying any guns in his vehicle.

"Then," reported Flores, "I heard gun-shots. . . . Rick reached toward the cop and I took off running. I heard about three or four shots."

Crime-scene evidence indicates that Enrique Casas first shot Officer Howell with a small handgun. When the officer fell to the ground, Casas then took Howell's .357 service revolver and shot him in the head.

Casas jumped in his car and drove off. Not far away, he picked up Sammy Flores.

"I asked Rick what happened," Flores told police.

"He said, 'I shot the cop.'

"I asked him what he did that for.

"He told me that if I didn't quit bugging him, he'd shoot me, too."

Enrique Casas subsequently fled to Mexico, where he has been sighted many times since 1986. He is also know to have run drugs back and forth between Mexico and Texas on several occasions. Besides the capital-murder warrant pending against him in Texas, a second, Mexican warrant also has been obtained by the Tarrant County and Fort Worth authorities. According to the Fort Worth police, under these rare dual warrants, if Casas is caught, he will be returned to Texas to stand trial for his life.

3. "Bang!"

ALVARO ISRAEL ALVARADO
Portland, Oregon

DATE OF BIRTH: DECEMBER 28, 1963
HEIGHT: FIVE FEET, FIVE INCHES
WEIGHT: 195 POUNDS
HAIR: BLACK
EYES: BROWN
ALSO KNOWN AS: "CHITO," LUIS MEDINA, ISRAEL
  SANDOVAL-ALVARADO, ISRAEL ALVARADO-SANDOVAL
REWARD: NONE
CONTACT: SERGEANT BUD JOHNSON
         MULTNOMAH COUNTY SHERIFF'S OFFICE
         PORTLAND, OREGON
         (503) 255-3600

Amanda Orozco Lima, common-law wife to hydrant-shaped Álvaro I. Alvarado, was a very frightened woman in the summer of 1989. She had just left her husband, fleeing with her two children from southern California to Portland, Oregon. Amanda knew that she had to stay hidden, because if Alvaro found her, he was apt to kill her.

She was dead right.

According to the Portland *Oregonian*, Álvaro and Amanda had been to the northwest together the previous year; they came north to

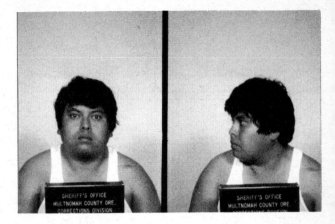

Álvaro Israel Alvarado

Portland where Álvaro sought employment. Whether he found any—or how he supported his little family—is not known. Detective Sergeant Bud Johnson of the Multnomah County Sheriff's Office guesses that Álvaro may have dabbled in drug dealing or transportation, although he has no drug arrest record. The only official notice taken of Álvaro Alvarado in 1988 was a Portland arrest for assaulting Amanda. Not long after the incident the common-law couple, both native Guatemalans, put the bulk of their possessions in storage and headed south again for California.

The next summer, Amanda finally summoned the courage to break away from Álvaro. She loaded their children—Alvaco, who was eight, and Berta, just nine months old—into the family car and drove back to Portland, where Ál-

varo's cousin, Otto Alvarado, worked as a part-
time free-lance disc jockey. Álvaro previously
had suspected Amanda of having an affair with
Otto.

Amanda arrived back in Portland in July 1989,
terrified that Álvaro would hunt her down. She
went so far as to repaint their car so that he
couldn't spot the vehicle on the street. And
when she rented a two-bedroom apartment for
herself and the kids, she told the building manager, June Lambert, to say nothing should anyone come looking for her.

There was one weak point in Amanda's security, however; her sister Gloria Orozco Lima. As
Detective Johnson has pieced the story together, "Álvaro laid a line on Gloria that
Amanda was sick and he wanted her to go up
and be with her sister. What happened was that
he and she came up to Portland together, and
then somehow he was able to follow her, or
Otto, to Amanda's apartment."

Álvaro did not confront Amanda immediately. Instead, he checked into a Portland motel
and bided his time until the night of August 15,
1989, a Thursday. Early that evening, Gloria
Orozco, together with Otto Alvarado and another, unnamed male, gathered at Amanda's for
a few hours of television and conversation. Little Alvaco played on the living-room floor as the
adults chatted. Berta was in the apartment as
well.

About ten o'clock, says Detective Johnson,
"Álvaro just opened the door and came in. There
was a conversation with Amanda in which she
basically told him she didn't want him there.
She then went for the telephone in the back

bedroom and he blocked her and kind of gave her a shove. At this point, her sister Gloria jumped up and confronted him physically, and verbally.

"He pushes her back and *bang!* shoots her in the chest with his .357. Then *bang!* he shoots Amanda twice. By this time Otto was coming up off the couch to try to take him and *bang! bang!* again."

All three victims were DOA at the hospital. The fourth member of the party, the unnamed male, escaped out the door just ahead of Álvaro's sixth and last shot, discharged from the living room and through the front window. This witness is now under the Multnomah County sheriff's protection.

The two Alvarado children were not harmed. Within a week of the shooting a Portland grand jury returned a multicount indictment for aggravated murder against Álvaro Alvarado, who faces a life sentence if convicted of the killings.

But first Bud Johnson has to catch his suspect. "This guy could be living anywhere," says Johnson. "He could easily be in southern California. He could be in Mexico. He could be back in Guatemala."

The appropriate law enforcement agencies in all these areas have been informed of Detective Johnson's interest in Alvarado, as has the U.S. Customs Service and the Border Patrol. All have been provided copies of his mugshot.

But as is usually true of fugitives, the longer Álvaro Alvarado remains at large, the more Detective Johnson will have to hope his quarry makes a mistake or gets a bad break. "It's really not that hard to commit a crime sometimes and disappear into the woodwork," he told reporter Holley Gilbert of the *Oregonian*. "[But Alvarado] might be going down the Santa Monica Freeway [someday] and blow a tire and a cop may stop and ask if he needs help. Then the cop may ask to see his driver's license, and maybe he won't have one."

4. Two Pounds of Speed

VINCENT LEGREND WALTERS
San Diego, California

DATE OF BIRTH: DECEMBER 10, 1966
HEIGHT: SIX FEET
WEIGHT: 170 POUNDS
HAIR: BROWN
EYES: BROWN
DISTINGUISHING MARKS OR SCARS: SCAR OVER LEFT EYE.
ALSO KNOWN AS: ''TAPE''
REWARD: UNDETERMINED AMOUNT
      CONTACT: SAN DIEGO CRIMESTOPPERS
      (619) 531-2373
      OR
      CHULA VISTA POLICE DEPARTMENT
      (619) 691-5202

In 1988, at age twenty-one, Vincent Legrend Walters was a thug on the way to the top of his class. His criminal past included a conviction in Colorado for second-degree burglary and pending charges in California for burglary and for assaulting a police officer with a deadly weapon. Vincent's future seemed assured in the southern California illegal drug trade. He was already a major player with close blood ties to Mexico's powerful Rafael Caro-Quintero crime family, and his methamphetamine manufacture

21

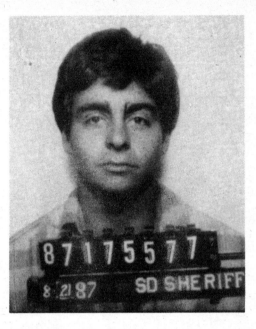

Vincent Legrend Walters

and distribution business in the San Diego area was worth tens of millions of dollars in profits, according to federal officials.

This robust operation began to unravel, however, in September of 1988 when Walters bought a substantial volume of raw drug-laboratory chemicals from Triple Neck Scientific in Kearny Mesa, California. Triple Neck Scientific, he soon learned, was a U.S. Drug Enforcement Administration front operation, and the feds were preparing to put Vincent out of business.

As rumors of a DEA raid on his lab grew stronger, Walters gave two pounds of his product—worth about $70,000 on the street—to an associate for safekeeping. According to officials of the San Diego Police Department's Fugitive Apprehension Unit, Vincent's friend then passed the two pounds of methamphetamines to another individual, who quickly disappeared with the drug trove. Realizing his own imminent peril, the associate sought to hide out from Walters's vengeance.

Vincent and others in his group found their erring erstwhile confederate on September 25, say the police, and endeavored to torture from him the location of their missing dope. The best this man could offer was a guess that Walters should try a house in Imperial Beach, a suburban stretch of Chula Vista, California, between San Diego and the Mexican border.

Walters and his group arrived at this address armed with pistols, an M-16 military rifle and a shotgun. They discovered three persons at home, two men and a twenty-one-year-old woman, Kristine Reyes. After roughing up one of the males, the gang blindfolded, bound and gagged all three and drove off with them.

The two men were taken to Walters's drug laboratory and held for five days until the two pounds of methamphetamine were returned. Ms. Reyes, who was tall and slim, with brown eyes and long, dark brown hair she wore straight, was driven to a house in El Cajon, northwest of San Diego. There, on the same day that Vincent Walters recovered his drugs and released his hostages, Kristine Reyes was found dead in a bedroom. She was fully clothed in green, knitted stretch pants, a stone-washed jeans jacket and pink Danskin slippers. There were no signs of physical or sexual assault. An autopsy discovered that Kristine died from inhaling carbon tetrachloride (cleaning fluid) from her cloth gag.

Several arrests were soon made; Walters himself was held for a time before being released. Then, nine months later, on June 8, 1989, Vincent Legrend Walters was indicted on a host of federal drug and weapons charges. He disappeared soon thereafter and is believed to be hiding in the United States or in Mexico with the help of his Mexican gangster relatives.

5. Homicide at a Bootleg House

WINIFRED LEE NOBLE
Dallas, Texas

DATE OF BIRTH: JUNE 6, 1943
HEIGHT: FIVE FEET, NINE INCHES
WEIGHT: 145 POUNDS
HAIR: BLACK (PROCESSED)
EYES: BROWN
ALSO KNOWN AS: "SONNY"
REWARD: $1,000 FROM DALLAS CRIMESTOPPERS
CONTACT: DALLAS POLICE DEPARTMENT
 DETECTIVE J. E. GALLAGHER
 (214) 670-1633

Winifred isn't much of a name for a career out-law. So Mr. Noble, a native of McKinney, Texas, just north of Dallas, calls himself "Sonny." His rap sheet extends back over decades and in-cludes arrests and convictions for a broad range of felonies from burglary to forgery and theft. He has served many short stints behind bars in city, county and state lockups. When Noble is at large, as he is now, he is known to seek work as a laborer. He customarily lives out of his au-tomobile, often with a female companion.

Back in 1985, about the only person in the

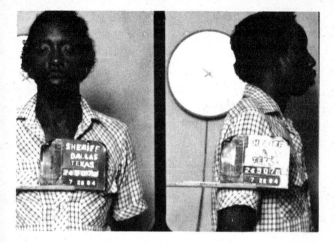

Winifred Lee Noble

Dallas neighborhood of south Oak Cliff who knew this much about Winifred was his girlfriend. As far as anyone else was concerned, Winifred Noble was just another guy who called himself "Sonny."

He liked to hang out in what are called "bootleg houses" in Oak Cliff. Due to strong local Baptist influence, the sale of liquor is banned in this largely black community. As a result, entrepreneurs open illegal bootleg houses in Oak Cliff. These are a modern version of the old speakeasies, residential properties furnished with a few couches, maybe a pool table, a jukebox and video games, where Oak Cliff's nonteetotaling citizens can buy liquor by the drink or bottle. Bootleg houses also sometimes offer hookers for their male clientele.

It was in one such establishment on the night of January 22, 1985, that Noble and his girlfriend got into an altercation with a man named Odell Livingston, who was there with a date. Witnesses told police that the argument suddenly escalated. "Sonny," as they knew him, pulled a handgun and put two fatal slugs into Livingston. Meantime, Noble's girlfriend produced a knife and slashed Livingston's date. Then Noble and his companion ran out the door, jumped in his green 1974 Mercury Cougar and drove away into the night.

Because Noble had been so secretive about his identity, it required several months for Dallas homicide detectives to establish who the shooter was. In the end, they had to lean on his girlfriend, a parole violator, to get the truth of who allegedly blew away Odell Livingston.

After the crime, Noble was reported in both Mississippi and Louisiana, but there have been no other sightings since 1986. The Dallas police warn that Noble probably is armed and that he is known to have bragged that he'll shoot anyone, cop or civilian, who tries to bring him in.

6. "We'll Catch Him"

RUBÉN ESCOBAR SÁNCHEZ
Yakima, Washington

DATE OF BIRTH: MAY 16, 1965
HEIGHT: FIVE FEET, SEVEN INCHES
WEIGHT: 147 POUNDS
HAIR: BLACK
EYES: BROWN
ALSO KNOWN AS: RUBÉN SÁNCHEZ ESCOBAR
REWARD: $5,000
CONTACT: YAKIMA COUNTY SHERIFF'S OFFICE
        DETECTIVE DAVID JOHNSON
        (509) 575-4080
        OR
        (800) 572-0490 (Inside Washington)

There was bad blood between Rubén Escobar Sánchez and Fidel Ruiz. Those who knew the two migrant farm workers later told Yakima, Washington, sheriff's detectives that the source of the friction was Rubén Sánchez's wife. Though pregnant with her fourth child by Rubén, she was the (presumably) innocent object of Fidel's persistent sexual interest. And since the would-be adulterer—who had a wife and children of his own in Mexico—wouldn't take no for an answer, Rubén finally decided

Rubén Escobar Sánchez
*(Photo courtesy David Johnson,
Yakima County Sheriff's Office)*

upon a permanent solution to the problem of
Fidel's passion for his wife. According to his indictment, he murdered Ruiz on August 24, 1989.

Sánchez chose as the site for the killing an empty
house situated in a cornfield owned by Ralph W.
Boyle, forty-five, a local farmer. Apparently, he
persuaded Ruiz to drive him out to the vacant
structure late in the afternoon of the twenty-
fourth. At about 7:00 P.M., Ralph Boyle was working on his tractor not far from the house when he
heard gunshots fired within it. Then smoke began
to curl up from the frame building, and Ralph
Boyle realized to his acute chagrin that someone
had just set the structure afire.

He steered the tractor toward his burning building from which Boyle soon spied Sánchez sprinting to Fidel Ruiz's car. Also, in the distance, Ralph saw his brother, Lane Boyle, driving along the road in their pickup truck. He flagged down Lane and together they drove off in pursuit of Sánchez.

The Boyles caught up with the fugitive about two miles down the road, directly in front of their friend and neighbor Stan Arquette's house. They forced Rubén to a stop and used their pickup as a blockade. The brothers then angrily approached Sánchez from the front of his vehicle. Ralph walked to the right. As he came athwart the driver's door, Rubén Sánchez drew his gun and shot at Boyle twice, through a rolled-up window. One bullet caught the farmer in the arm and the other slammed into Boyle's head. He dropped where he stood, mortally wounded.

As Ralph Boyle fell, Rubén Sánchez tried to back up his car to escape. But Lane Boyle had already leaped into the pickup again. Although Sánchez shot once more and hit Lane once in the hand, Boyle was able to ram the stolen car and disable it.

All the racket, shouts and gunfire brought Stan Arquette to his front door, where he promptly started blasting away at Sánchez with his .357. Rubén scrambled away from the now-useless car and ran down the road about a hundred yards to another house. He burst in on the startled family, waving his handgun and demanding the keys to their car. Informed that the keys were in the auto's ignition, Sanchez ran back out, climbed into the vehicle and sped away under a fresh fusillade from Stan Arquette, who had brought out his rifle for longer-range salvos.

Arquette hit the disappearing vehicle twice. Rubén Sánchez, who never had been arrested for anything more serious than minor motor-vehicle violations, had now gunned down two men in the space of a few minutes, and injured a third. He drove home in his second stolen car of the day, gathered up his wife and their pre-school children and a few belongings and took off that night in the family's 1978 yellow Chevy Caprice station wagon. They rested overnight with relatives in Wapato, Washington, south-east of Yakima. The next morning, as Yakima authorities were raking Fidel Ruiz's charred bones out of the Boyleses' burned house, the five Sanchezes headed south for Ontario, California, directly east of Los Angeles, where the children were left in the care of Rubén's sister.

After they had unloaded the kids, one of the Sánchezes' more obvious possible destinations was his native Mexico, which has no extradition treaty with the United States. But Rubén Sánchez had to be careful not to return to his Mexican hometown, where Fidel Ruiz had relatives too. As Yakima detective David Johnson explained to reporter Thomas P. Skeen of the Yakima *Herald-Republic:* "Fidel's family said that if they found Sánchez, they'd ship his body back in a bag."

In December of 1989, four months after the killings, Rubén's brother brought the three Sánchez children back up from southern California to Yakima County to live with him. Subsequently, there have been unconfirmed sightings of Rubén and his wife in the area. Despite the many serious charges against him—two counts of first-degree murder, one count of second-degree arson, one count of first-degree assault and one count of first-degree theft—Rubén Sánchez may be willing to run the risk just to see his kids occasionally.

If he is that daring, says Detective Johnson, then Sánchez will hasten the moment of his inevitable capture. "We'll catch him," an assured Johnson has told the *Herald-Republic*. "He's going to feel confident. He's going to get cocky and make a mistake."

7. A Dangerous Liaison

ROBERT THOMAS CHICKENE
Missoula, Montana

DATE OF BIRTH: NOVEMBER 3, 1950
HEIGHT: SIX FEET
WEIGHT: 170 POUNDS
HAIR: REDDISH BLOND
EYES: BLUE
ALSO KNOWN AS: TOM SPENCE, "SPORTSTER BOB"
OTHER: ASSOCIATES WITH BANDITOS AND GHOST RIDERS MOTORCYCLE GANGS
REWARD: FIVE VALLEY CRIMESTOPPERS OF MISSOULA, MONTANA, OFFER UP TO $5,000 FOR INFORMATION LEADING TO CHICKENE'S ARREST.
CONTACT: LIEUTENANT DON MORMAN
         MISSOULA COUNTY SHERIFF
         (406) 721-5700, EXT. 3314

Paula Squires Rodriguez of Missoula, Montana, was born in 1963 and lived for twenty-two years. She was married once (and briefly) to Randy Rodriguez and bore a child who died of birth defects.

The last nine months of Paula's abruptly abbreviated life began in January of 1985 when she met a biker and drug dealer who called himself Tom Spence, but who was informally known to his fellow bikers as "Sportster Bob,"

Robert Thomas Chickene
*(Photos courtesy Don Morman,
Missoula County Sheriff's Office)*

after the Harley-Davidson motorcycle model he operated. Ms. Rodriguez and "Tom Spence" started dating early in 1985. Soon they were living together in a house he was buying at 1106 Cooper Street in Missoula. Around the corner on Scott Street resided his friend, also a biker and a tattoo-shop owner called "Scootin' Newton."

"At first," Paula's mother Carolyn Squires later said of "Tom Spence" to a TV reporter, "he took her to dinner. He bought her flowers. At one point, she showed [her sister] Barbara that he'd put some stocks in her name." Mrs. Squires also recalled in her television interview how Paula delighted in her boyfriend's attentions. "See, Mom," she would say, "he really cares." Genuine affection from males apparently had been unusual in Paula's experience.

In time, however, the romance began to sour. Paula, who was given to wild tantrums, started quarreling with her lover. Mrs. Squires noticed bruises on her. A friend confirmed that "Tom Spence" had beaten Paula.

Such was the frayed state of their once-dreamy relationship when in mid-September of 1985 "Sportster Bob" and Paula took off on a motorcycle trip. By this time, Ms. Rodriguez also knew his real name wasn't Tom Spence, but Robert T. Chickene, and that Chickene, a New York State native, was wanted by federal agents in connection with a vacation travel scam he'd operated out of a boiler room in Las Vegas.

It was dangerous for Paula to know these things.

On the twenty-third of September, she called

home from Spokane, Washington, to her mother in Missoula to say that she expected to be back within a day. Paula was excited to hear from Mrs. Squires that her dog had just had puppies.

When her daughter didn't telephone from the Cooper Street house the next day, Carolyn Squires drove by and spoke to Sportster Bob, who told her that they had returned the previous night as anticipated, but that he and Paula had fought violently. Paula, he related, marched out of the house, supposedly to go buy a pack of cigarettes, and as yet had not returned.

Nine days later, there was still no sign of Paula Squires Rodriguez. On October 2, 1985, a very worried Carolyn Squires reported her daughter missing to the Missoula County Sheriff's Office.

A uniformed deputy, Larry Jacobs, took Mrs. Squires's report and then went to 1106 Cooper, where he discovered the living-room rug being removed and some painting being done. "Tom Spence" explained that he was fixing up the place in order to sell it. He offered Officer Jacobs no new information, but he did alter his story. Instead of Paula leaving in a huff in search of cigarettes, "Tom Spence" now confided that he had thrown her out of the house that night.

Several weeks passed. Mrs. Squires kept hounding the sheriff's office to mount a more active investigation into her daughter's disappearance. In response, Lieutenant Don Morman assigned Detective Stanley Fullerton to the case. Fullerton notified the appropriate national agencies that Paula Rodriguez was a missing person, and he began making detective-type in-

inquiries around town. On the thirty-first—
Halloween—Fullerton visited the house on Cooper Street. A young woman came to the door and
told him "Mr. Spence" was not around. In fact,
Bob Chickene had moved his gear from 1106
and was living around the corner on Scott
Street with his buddy, Scootin' Newton.

"Chickene," explains Lieutenant Morman,
"wanted to distance himself from that house.
He got this floozy that he met and she started
living in there. He's kind of transient now, moving his stuff to Scootin' Newton's."

However, Chickene had not lost his cool.
When Detective Fullerton returned to his office
that day, the telephone was ringing. It was
"Tom Spence."

"You want to talk to me?" Chickene asked.
"I'll come up to the office."

Which he did.

"Pretty brazen!" observes Lieutenant Morman. "Here's a guy wanted by the feds on thirteen counts and he comes up to our office and
has a conversation with Fullerton for about a
half hour. He said, 'I don't know what the hell
happened to her. She just kind of left.'"

The next day, a Friday, a Spokane police officer out elk hunting along a logging road in the
mountains about thirty-five miles west of Missoula noticed some brush and a tarp covering
an elongated object lying in a shallow creek bed.
The cop walked over, pulled back the tarp and
discovered a dead female on her back in the
cold-running water. She had been shot in the
upper torso. Three days later, the body was
identified as that of Paula Squires Rodriguez.

By Friday, November 8, 1985, the Missoula

sheriff's office had obtained search warrants for both the Cooper Street house and Scootin' Newton's around the corner on Scott. Since this was an election year, the local press was invited along to record Missoula's law enforcement dollars at work. Among the material confiscated on that date was a variety of drugs and drug-related paraphernalia.

Bob Chickene was not at either house. According to what the sheriff's office later was able to learn, he had been with pals at a motorcycle shop just outside of town. That evening, Chickene turned on the repair-shop television set to watch the ten o'clock news and watched in astonishment the taped coverage of the police raid on his and Scootin' Newton's addresses.

Chickene reacted quickly. Before the sports report was over, he was riding southeast out of town, out of the county and out of the state. He was in such a hurry that Chickene even left his Sportster behind.

Witnesses and anonymous calls to the Five Valley Crimestoppers' number enabled the Missoula County Sheriff's Office to establish the probable circumstances of Paula Rodriguez's murder. Lieutenant Morman believes Chickene shot and killed Paula in the Cooper Street house late on September 23, or in the early-morning hours of the twenty-fourth. The fugitive's flashpoint was reached, said witnesses, when Paula threatened to expose him to the police. Based on this and other evidence that the sheriff will not disclose, Chickene has been charged with one count of so-called deliberate homicide in

Montana, the gravest charge possible in that state.

Further investigation revealed that "Tom Spence" was a deceased elderly black man who had lived in Florida. Chickene acquired Spence's social security number and other identification in the course of being a fugitive from the federal charges in Las Vegas.

He is thought to have fled to New Orleans, where he remained for some time. There is reason to believe that Chickene then moved on to Arizona and up to Las Vegas again. His trail apparently goes cold after that, although the Missoula sheriff advises that Bob Chickene may also have visited Utah, Idaho, Washington and even Montana over the past few years.

8. Hitman

DALE PATRICK PALMER
Dallas, Texas

DATE OF BIRTH: FEBRUARY 25, 1964
HEIGHT: FIVE FEET, TEN INCHES
WEIGHT: 155 POUNDS
HAIR: BLACK
EYES: BROWN
ALSO KNOWN AS: ''BLACKA''
REWARD: $1,000 FROM DALLAS CRIMESTOPPERS
CONTACT: DALLAS POLICE DEPARTMENT
        DETECTIVE J. F. ALLISON
        (214) 670-1633

According to the Dallas, Texas, Police Department, Dale Patrick Palmer is a killer in the hire of Jamaican drug gangs, or "posses" as they also are known. These Jamaican customers, say the police, keep the twenty-six-year-old native Trinidadian so busy on his various murder missions around the country that Palmer really has no known permanent residence. "He flies around and takes care of business for them," explains Dallas homicide detective J. E. Gallagher. "A guy like this can be killing somebody here at noon and be on the streets of New York City by six."

Most of Palmer's work appears to be enforce-

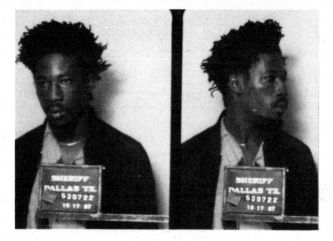

Dale Patrick Palmer

ment. Many crack dealers in Dallas, for example, are New York City ghetto teenagers lured to Texas by the promise of a big score. When they find out that they're going to make, at most, $200 a week operating crack houses, some of the youngsters start to steal or free-lance. Once they are detected, hitmen such as Dale Palmer are brought in to shoot the kids. "They don't get any second chances," observes Detective Gallagher, who knows of at least sixteen such cases over the past three years in Dallas. Most recently, he investigated a shooting in which the offending crack dealer's hands were nailed to a table before he was shot in the kneecaps and then in his head.

Dale Palmer first came to the Dallas Police Department's attention on October 10, 1988, when he shot and wounded a drug dealer in the city's Oak Cliff district. An off-duty cop witnessed the shooting and chased Palmer into an alley, where he arrested him. Palmer was carrying a nine-millimeter Smith & Wesson with eight rounds in the chamber. He also had three-tenths of a gram of marijuana in his pocket.

A year later, Dale Palmer's name surfaced again, this time in connection with the murder of a south Dallas used-car salesman named James Farmer. According to what detectives have been able to learn, Farmer had the bad luck to have mishandled an auto loan deal involving one of Dale Palmer's close friends. Vengeance therefore is a possible explanation for the events of a few days later—Halloween night, 1989. Palmer, out driving around Dallas with three friends, saw Farmer in his car and allegedly swerved in front of the car dealer, forcing Farmer to stop.

Otis Ramsey, sitting in on the passenger side of Farmer's vehicle, later told police that Palmer (whom Ramsey would identify in a photo lineup) exited his car, walked over to Farmer—still buckled in his driver's seat—and casually squeezed a lethal round into his head.

The same evening, another black man named Charles Howard, age thirty-four, was shot in the right eye just blocks from where Farmer was murdered. Later ballistic tests indicated to a certainty that the same .44- or .45-caliber weapon had been used in both shootings.

Based for the most part on Otis Ramsey's eyewitness identification, Dale Patrick Palmer was formally charged with James Farmer's murder on December 14, 1989. It had taken nerve for

Ramsey to finger an accused killer such as Palmer, a brave moment that he soon began to rue. According to the Dallas police, Ramsey later telephoned Farmer's widow to say he was afraid to testify against her husband's killer in court.

Then violence struck again.

On February 27, 1990, Otis Ramsey and some vagrants were sharing a fire and a bottle of wine in a vacant lot, also near where James Farmer had died. Two men approached. "Hey Otis," one of them called, "come over here." The rest of the group at the fire remember Otis Ramsey doing as he was asked. Ramsey talked to the two men for a short while and then turned back toward the fire. That was when one of the strangers fired two bullets in the back of Otis Ramsey's head.

NOTE: *Dale Patrick Palmer was apprehended in late May, 1990, by the Dallas police. At the time, he described himself as unemployed but declined to accept the assistance of a court-appointed attorney. Instead, Palmer hired his own local lawyer, and, as of mid-July, remained free on $50,000 bond.*

9. Arson

THE VÁSQUEZ BROTHERS
El Paso, Texas

HUMBERTO RIVAS

DATE OF BIRTH: EARLY 1962
HEIGHT: FIVE FEET, THREE INCHES
WEIGHT: 145 POUNDS
HAIR: BROWN
EYES: BROWN

OMAR ADRIÁN

DATE OF BIRTH: JANUARY 1, 1963
HEIGHT: FIVE FEET, SIX INCHES
WEIGHT: 146 POUNDS
HAIR: BLACK
EYES: BROWN
DISTINGUISHING MARKS OR SCARS: MOLES ON CHIN AND RIGHT CHEEK
ALSO KNOWN AS: ARTURO COY PAREDES, CARLOS RAMÍREZ
REWARD: EL PASO CRIMESTOPPERS OFFERS $1,000. FOR INFORMATION LEADING TO THE ARREST OF THE VÁSQUEZ BROTHERS.
CONTACT: EL PASO CRIMESTOPPERS
(915) 543-6000
OR
DETECTIVE ANTONIO E. LEYBA
HOMICIDE SECTION

Humberto Vásquez

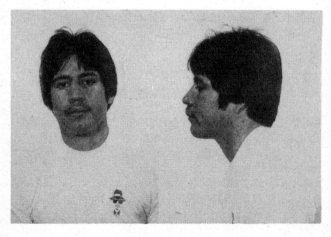

Omar Vásquez

EL PASO POLICE DEPARTMENT
(915) 564-7024

Humberto and Omar Vásquez, Mexican nationals formerly of El Paso, Texas, were a rambunctious pair, fond of beer, sniffing glue and very loud music, which they inflicted nearly nightly on their neighbors at the twenty-unit Alexandra Apartments on the corner of North Oregon and Arizona streets in downtown El Paso. Their mother, Margarita, who lived with them in the one-bedroom, $155-a-month apartment, could not, or would not, rein in her sons. Practically every night after Omar got home from his job as a busboy and Humberto returned from his work, washing dishes, the brothers would turn up their radio, crack open a few beers and then party until well past three in the morning.

Their neighbors' complaints did not faze them, nor did several stern admonitions to tone it down from the Alexandra's manager, Matías Chasco. Finally, Chasco evicted all three Vásquezes in May of 1982.

The brothers took the manager's action strongly amiss; witnesses reported that they vowed revenge on Chasco. One, a woman who lived at the Alexandra, later told police she'd heard Humberto and Omar plotting to blow up the place.

Nothing happened for four months. Then, on the night of September 24, a suspicious fire broke out near Matías Chasco's apartment on the second floor of the seventy-three-year-old,

three-story Alexandra complex. The blaze soon
burned out of control and ultimately gutted the
structure. Six third-floor residents perished as
a result of the fire—five adults and a four-year-
old boy—and sixteen others were injured. It was
the worst such tragedy in El Paso's history.

Humberto and Omar Vásquez immediately
became prime suspects. A witness allegedly saw
one of the Vásquez boys pouring generous
quantities of a flammable fluid onto the hallway
floor in front of manager Chasco's apartment.
(Chasco, it turned out, was not home that night.)
Others were able to place the Vásquezes lurking about the building on the night of the
twenty-fourth. Early the next morning both
brothers fled into Mexico; Humberto did not
even bother to pick up his paycheck from the
restaurant where he worked.

Neither Humberto nor Omar had a history of
arrests or violent behavior, including fire setting. "The Vásquezes weren't considered dangerous [by the police] at that time," says
Detective Antonio Leyba of the El Paso Police
Department, who has been on the case from the
start. "They probably didn't even mean to burn
the place down. They probably just wanted to
scare the manager."

The prank, if that is what it was meant to be,
netted the Vásquez boys six capital-murder indictments each in October 1982. If convicted in
a Texas court of the arson homicides, they
would face a maximum penalty of death by lethal injection. Needless to say, neither brother
has returned to face U.S. justice, although Detective Leyba says they've been seen at least
once in Arizona and periodically reported in the

El Paso vicinity, most recently in April of 1988. It is possible—although not likely—that Humberto and Omar will someday be arrested in Mexico. If so, they cannot be extradited to Texas, but could be tried in a Mexican court, where the stiffest sentence for their alleged crimes is thirty years in prison.

SECTION TWO

CENTRAL

1. Mom and Dad

WILLIAM LESLIE ARNOLD
Omaha, Nebraska

DATE OF BIRTH: AUGUST 28, 1942
HEIGHT: FIVE FEET, TEN INCHES
WEIGHT: APPROXIMATELY 160 POUNDS
HAIR: DARK BROWN
EYES: BROWN
DISTINGUISHING MARKS OR SCARS: SCARS ON FOREHEAD, LEFT ARM AND RIGHT CHEEK
REWARD: THE NEBRASKA STATE PATROL AND NEBRASKA CRIMESTOPPERS WILL PAY UNSPECIFIED SUMS FOR INFORMATION LEADING TO APPREHENSION. CALL CRIMESTOPPERS (INSIDE NEBRASKA ONLY) (800) 422-1495
CONTACT: NEBRASKA STATE PATROL
         SERGEANT DAN SCOTT
         (402) 471-4545

When reporters talked to Leslie Arnold's teachers at Central High School in Omaha, Nebraska, they were told that the sixteen-year-old junior was a quiet, well-behaved boy who played the clarinet and tenor saxophone, did fairly well in class and was rarely absent. Others, however, knew him as a willful, delinquent juvenile, "a high-strung, flighty boy," according to his uncle Ben McCammon, and a terror to the other kids in the middle-class district where

William Leslie Arnold
(Journal-Star Printing Co.)

he was raised. One local adolescent told the Lincoln (Nebraska) *Journal* that Leslie Arnold was feared for his violent temper, that with slight provocation he had recently tried to throttle this youth's younger brother.

This was in the autumn of 1958, and the reason that the Nebraska press was asking questions about Leslie's nature was that the boy had just been charged with murdering both his parents.

The crimes occurred in the late afternoon of September 27, a Saturday. As Leslie later explained in his confession, his mother, forty-year-old Opel Arnold, had caught her older son in an untruth about three weeks earlier, and as punishment had forbade Leslie access to either of the family cars. He had also been in trouble with his parents for monopolizing the family telephone with calls to his girlfriend, whom Leslie was determined to take to the drive-in movie the night of the twenty-seventh.

Mrs. Arnold would not hear of it. So her boy went upstairs and came back with a .22 semiautomatic rifle. He squeezed six shots into his mom's heart as she stood in her dining room. His dad, William Arnold, forty-two, came home a short time later and discovered Mrs. Arnold dead on the floor. According to Leslie, Mr. Arnold tried to grab him but missed, and then Leslie shot his dad, too, six times in the chest.

Leslie wrapped his parents' blood-caked corpses in an eight-by-ten rug and dragged them down into the basement. Back upstairs, he mopped up the remainder of their blood with two of Mrs. Arnold's small throw rugs. These, together with the larger rug, he later tossed into a nearby creek.

The teenager next took a shower and changed his clothes. Then he climbed in the family car and drove into the huge Ak-Sar-Ben (that's Nebraska spelled backward) Racetrack across the street, where his younger brother, Jimmie Arnold, worked as an usher. Leslie told Jimmie that their parents had decided on the spur of the moment to go visit relatives in Loup City, Nebraska, a small town on the Middle Loup River in Sherman County, about 150 miles due west of Omaha. While Mr. and Mrs. Arnold were away, Leslie said, Jimmie was to stay with Uncle Ben's family, which Leslie already had arranged. He drove Jimmie over to Uncle Ben's that evening and then picked up his girlfriend and went to the movies.

The next morning, Leslie borrowed a neighbor's shovel, explaining that his parents wanted him to do some work in the garden. That night, with brother Jimmie conveniently removed to Uncle Ben's house, Leslie carried William and Opel up from the basement and buried them under three feet of dirt in their backyard flower bed, near a lilac bush.

Leslie's story of his parents' sudden departure stood up for a few days. Then neighbors and relatives, including Uncle Ben McCammon, began to wonder what was going on. Calls to Loup City established that the Arnolds had not arrived there. The Omaha police were provided a missing persons' report.

A week later, the boy's paternal grandparents drove to Omaha from their house in North Loup, Nebraska (northeast of Loup City). They, too, stayed with Ben McCammon and his family while Leslie continued on alone at home.

By this time, Uncle Ben and other relatives harbored dark fears of foul play, and some family members had a suspect in mind. They noted that Leslie was conducting himself with uncommon civility ever since his parents' disappearance. That made Ben McCammon especially suspicious. On Friday night, October 11, thirteen days after the Arnolds last were seen alive, McCammon called a family council to be held at the Arnold house. Leslie skipped the meeting for a high-school football game that evening.

"We felt we'd waited long enough," McCammon explained to the Omaha *World-Tribune*. "Mrs. Arnold [Leslie and Jimmie's grandmother] didn't want to call in the police. The rest of the family kind of overpowered her. It's lucky we did." In the midst of these discussions, Leslie Arnold came home from the football game. His aunts and uncles told him what they intended to do. According to McCammon, "he seemed totally unconcerned."

On Saturday morning, October 11, the police put Leslie Arnold through a more focused interrogation than they had before, and this time the teenager confessed what he had done. According to the Lincoln *Journal*, Leslie took the police to his parents' graves in the flower garden and stood by impassively as first Opel, and then William, were exhumed. Mrs. Arnold's feet were bound with a leather belt. The boy's only outward sign of emotion at the gravesite came when a neighbor lady looked at him and said in disbelief, "Oh, Leslie! How could you do it?"

The *Journal* said that the question prompted
Leslie Arnold's lower lip to quiver.

The only other feeling that Leslie is said to
have shown at any time after his confession was
fright, expressed by tears, when his bond was
denied. He was otherwise stonily aloof at his
arraignment and did not betray any emotion
when he was charged with two counts of first-
degree murder for brutally gunning down his
mother and father. He pleaded innocent to the
allegations and was held in the county jail until
June of 1959, when he agreed to a second-
degree-murder plea bargain. He was sentenced
to two lifetimes in the Nebraska State Peniten-
tiary.

Eight years later, on July 15, 1967, Arnold
broke out of the state pen with another murderer, thirty-two-year-old James Harding. As
their escape was later reconstructed, the pair
cut through a set of bars in a hobby-room window. Sometime after six o'clock that night, they
slipped through the window and up over a
twelve-foot fence to freedom.

The next day a motorist reported seeing two
men clad in prison-issue and answering Arnold
and Harding's descriptions prowling around a
farm machine shed near the town of Pickell,
thirty-two miles southeast of Lincoln. Eighty
cops and prison employees descended on the
rugged, swampy countryside. They combed it,
inch by inch, under a brutal sun with great
clouds of mosquitoes rising up from fetid creek
bottoms to sting them. The search went on for
two days before the authorities gave up in despair. Several months later, the Lincoln *Journal*
paraphrased warden Maurice Sigler's charac-

terization of the escape as "one of the cleanest getaways in his experience."

The following year, James Harding was recaptured in Los Angeles. Nebraska law enforcement officials have had no such luck with Leslie Arnold, who has successfully eluded them now for more than twenty-three years. They warn that it is prudent to consider Arnold armed and dangerous.

2. "A Vicious Woman"

NORMA BAKER
Detroit, Michigan

DATE OF BIRTH: SOMETIME IN 1930
HEIGHT: FIVE FEET, NINE INCHES
WEIGHT: 220 POUNDS
HAIR: BROWN
EYES: BROWN
DISTINGUISHING MARKS OR SCARS: TWO SMALL MOLES UN-
    DER LEFT EAR, ONE SMALL MOLE UNDER LIP
OTHER: EXTREMELY HEAVY SMOKER
REWARD: NONE
CONTACT: DETROIT POLICE DEPARTMENT
            HOMICIDE DEPARTMENT
            (313) 596-2260

James Baker, at age fifty, was tired—tired of Detroit, tired of the hassles involved with managing his diverse and lucrative real-estate properties in the city and very tired of his fat, money-grubbing and mean-spirited wife, Norma. "Divorce me," he told her, "and you can have everything we own. Just give me $50,000. All I want is to get out of here and go home to Alabama and fish."

Norma had another idea. Her husband's life was heavily insured; "Jay," as he was known, was worth considerably more to her dead than

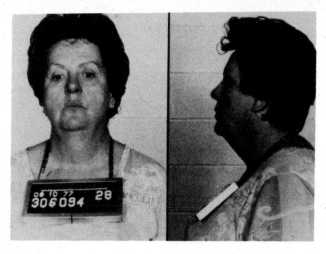

Norma Baker

alive, or divorced or any other way. Rather than pay him $50,000 to go home, she thought, why not pay someone a lot less to kill him? So she found a hitman named Norman Richardson and gave him $1,000 to kill Jay—half on signing and half when the job was done.

At one o'clock on the afternoon of May 12, 1977, Jay and his brother-in-law John Floyd Moore drove up the alleyway behind one of Baker's buildings with a load of windowpanes. Out stepped Norman Richardson to shoot both of them dead. Unfortunately for Mr. Richardson and Mrs. Baker, a tenant in the building, Bobby Bowman, was an eyewitness to the slayings. At trial, Bowman's testimony was crucial in establishing to a jury's satisfaction that

Norma and Norman were guilty of conspiracy to commit murder, first-degree murder and second-degree murder.

Justice seemed to have been served. Then came reporter James G. Tittsworth's piece in the April 9, 1981, editions of the *Detroit News:*

JAILER IRATE OVER
ESCAPE OF MURDERER

Wayne County's jail administrator promised "heads are going to roll" after the escape of a Detroit woman who was to have been sentenced today for the slayings of her former husband and his brother-in-law.

The escapee, Norma Baker, 52, had a trusty status at the jail's annex . . . despite facing a mandatory life sentence for first-degree murder.

"She had been convicted of first-degree murder, conspiracy to commit murder and second-degree murder," said Frank Wilkerson, jail administrator. "She is a vicious woman and putting her in a trusty status is unconscionable."

Mrs. Baker escaped Tuesday night while she was supposed to be cleaning offices at the sheriff department's road patrol and investigation offices, about a block from the annex.

Unlike most other law enforcement agencies, the Detroit police refused to assist in compiling this profile of their fugitive killer. They also refused to comment on why Norma Baker has remained at large for so long, or where they think she might be.

3. ". . . I Got Away."

DAVID GORDON SMITH
Catoosa, Oklahoma

DATE OF BIRTH: AUGUST 23, 1953
HEIGHT: SIX FEET, THREE INCHES
WEIGHT: 193 POUNDS
HAIR: BROWN
EYES: HAZEL
DISTINGUISHING MARKS OR SCARS: BULLET SCARS ON LEFT
   HAND AND LEFT LEG. ALSO SCARS ON LEFT FOREARM AND
   RIGHT HAND.
OTHER: REQUIRES CORRECTIVE LENSES
REWARD: UNSPECIFIED AMOUNT
CONTACT: OKLAHOMA STATE DEPARTMENT OF CORRECTIONS
       ESCAPE TEAM: (405) 425-2568, OR 2570
       OR: CRIMESTOPPERS
       (405) 235-7300

The town of Catoosa in Rogers County, northeast of Tulsa, Oklahoma, is so small that it does not appear at all on some road maps. Catoosa's just the kind of quiet place attractive to itinerant criminals who figure they have a better chance going up against small-town justice than they do trying to foil big-city police departments.

That was one of the reasons that David Gordon Smith, twenty-five, and his accomplice, twenty-

David Gordon Smith

nine-year-old Jackie R. Young, came to Catoosa on September 1, 1978. The second reason was that Catoosa was home to an Oklahoma State auto-license agency. According to what prosecutors later learned, the two men figured to steal some tags and then set up a false-car-title business.

The heist might have gone smoothly that day had it not been Smith and Young's extraordinarily bad luck that one of the employees inside the agency was talking by phone with a relative as the two robbers walked in and pulled their guns.

The relative on the other end of the line was a police dispatcher, who instantly broadcast a "crime-in-progress" alert to all local law enforcement officers. One who heard the bulletin was sheriff's deputy J. B. Hamby, who was but three blocks from the license bureau. Within a minute Hamby was on the scene, handgun drawn.

J. B. Hamby was fearless, says Catoosa police chief Benny Dirck. "He was the type of guy that would have gone in there against fifty guns." Two were quite enough that day. Hamby stormed through the front door, saw several license-agency employees cowering on the floor and in the same moment took fire from Smith and Young. Hamby returned the robbers' shots, hitting both of them before stumbling back out the door, a .22 round from Smith's weapon buried in his chest. He made it next door to a laundry, where he called for an ambulance, then dropped and died.

Back inside the license bureau, the wounded Jackie Young decided it was time for him to check out too. Young turned his .357 on himself. David Smith, whom deputy Hamby had hit in the left hand and left leg, managed to escape to his girlfriend's place in Tulsa. Later in the day, however, her attempts to secure Smith some medical help attracted the police to her residence, where they took David into custody.

According to Rick Sitzman, a former Rogers County assistant district attorney who would help prosecute David Smith, when a Tulsa patrolman told the outlaw that his buddy was dead, Smith grinned and replied, "Yeah, but I got away." "Of course," says Sitzman, "that came back to haunt him at the trial, but it was just indicative of his attitude."

But David Gordon Smith, for all his cold-bloodedness, was not just another homegrown sociopath. He came from an upstanding Tulsa family (his father was a university professor) and David himself had attended Oklahoma State University. What is more, he was intelligent and uncannily manipulative.

Following his 1979 conviction and resultant life sentence for the murder of deputy Hamby, Smith was first sent to a maximum-security state prison. But he seemed such a mild and obliging inmate that six months later he was assigned to a medium-security facility at Stringtown. Two years after that, his record still unblemished, the killer was removed to the Jackie Brannon Correctional Facility, a minimum-security installation at McAlester.

Along the way, he was once allowed out to enter a Tulsa marathon. Other times, he was taken on escorted weekend fishing trips. David Smith, with official approval, also invested in residential property. He bought a house in Muskogee, the country-western singer Merle Haggard's hometown.

Prosecutor Sitzman understands Smith as an ultimate gamesman, someone who could even smile at having "won" by surviving the Catoosa shoot-out with detective Hamby, while his supposed friend Mr. Young didn't. If so, then perhaps the game of being a prisoner began to bore David Smith. On October 28, 1985, at the 1:00 A.M. bedcheck at the Jackie Brannon prison, David Gordon Smith was missing. And he is still missing. How he got out, and where he's gone, are complete mysteries. Oklahoma authorities suspect he may be in Mexico.

4. An Incompetent Thug

DONALD ANTHONY DURANT
Cleveland, Ohio

DATE OF BIRTH: SOMETIME IN 1938
HEIGHT: FIVE FEET, NINE INCHES
WEIGHT: 150 POUNDS
HAIR: BROWN
EYES: BLUE
DISTINGUISHING MARKS OR SCARS: TWO-INCH SCAR AT FOREHEAD HAIRLINE
OTHER: USES DISGUISES AND HAS HAD EXTENSIVE PLASTIC SURGERY. MAY BE ACCOMPANIED BY HIS GIRLFRIEND, JEANNE HAYES RODE, A FORMER DANCER AND COCKTAIL WAITRESS ALSO KNOWN AS JEANNE SIFFIN. MIGHT BE WORKING AS A BARTENDER, HOUSEPAINTER OR SALESMAN.
ALSO KNOWN AS: CARL BARONE, MARIO CAMPOLA, SAM RONALD CAMPOLA, MARIO DURANT, MIKE SANZO
REWARD: $2,000 FROM CLEVELAND CRIMESTOPPERS
CONTACT: CUYAHOGA COUNTY SHERIFF'S OFFICE
DETECTIVE TOM HITSMAN
OR
SERGEANT DON MESTER
(216) 443-6124

Some boys dream of becoming firemen. Others want to be ballplayers or doctors or cops. But

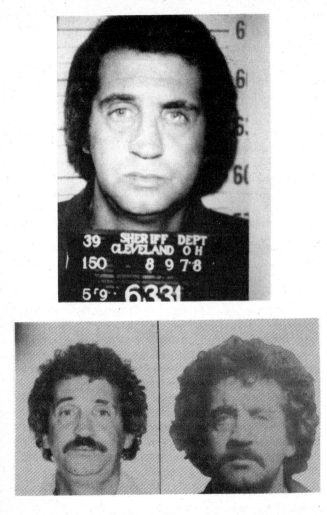

Donald Anthony Durant

not Donny Durant of Cleveland, Ohio. All he ever wanted to be was a thug.

That is what Lieutenant Chester M. Zembala, chief of detectives at the Cuyahoga County Sheriff's Office, claims. Durant's boyhood role models in the Collingwood district of east side Cleveland, says Zembala, were mostly Italian-American outlaws, his friends' fathers and uncles. Donald Durant even changed his given name to Mario to be more like his heroes. "Eventually," remarks the detective, "he probably wanted to get in the Mafia or something."

Durant's career aspirations have been thwarted, however, because Donald (or Mario) lacks what it takes to become a major-league gangster. "He isn't qualified," opines Zembala. "He isn't smart enough." Durant tried to dress the part, affecting all-white or all-black getups in emulation of TV hoods or the continental cat burglars he'd seen in the movies. In his case, however, clothes did not make the man. Donald Durant was doomed never to be a criminal of distinction.

As a youth, he did time at all the right reform schools as he worked on his specialty, housebreaking. Then Durant picked up a trade, interior painting, and parlayed the craft into a niche within a third-rate Collingwood-district gang of burglars. "Those guys made so many mistakes," explained Lieutenant Zembala, "I don't know how they ever stole anything."

Durant was their legman, the one who cased the targets. Posing as a painting contractor, he would approach home owners who were known, or imagined, to keep treasures at home. These prospective marks, innocently assuming that

Durant was legitimate, would show him around inside their houses, where he could note details important to the planning and execution of successful burglaries. Then he would report back to his colleagues and together they'd plan the caper.

It was in this capacity that Donald Durant set up a 1972 job at 15035 Alexander Road in Walton Hills, Ohio, then a bosky, lightly populated suburb of Cleveland. The address of Alexander Road belonged to two half-brothers, Dr. Clarence Porbe and Edwin Chapek, who was forty-nine-years-old at the time. Dr. Porbe was rumored to have an extensive and very valuable rare-coin collection that he kept in the house.

The Walton Hills village police first heard of trouble at 15035 Alexander Road at about 5:00 P.M. on May 24, 1972. Neighbor Joe Kluber telephoned breathlessly from his house next door to say that he had just driven his green truck into the Porbe–Chapek driveway and encountered a white male in a U-Haul van speeding up toward him from the house. The two vehicles nearly collided, he said.

Kluber, who had come to pick up Edwin Chapek, continued on down to the house and parked his truck. As he let himself into the residence, he was grabbed by two males, who took his wallet and forced him into the kitchen, where they ordered him to lie facedown on the floor. Just then a third male voice shouted, "He's gone! He's gone!" Kluber's captors bolted for the front door. Some moments later, Kluber himself ventured back outside to encounter utter stillness. Everyone and everything, including his green truck, was gone. He did not linger to look for Mr. Chapek, whose dead body was slumped on the ground not far away.

The action meantime had moved up the driveway and out onto Alexander Road. The U-Haul truck, witnesses later told police, immediately became mired in rush-hour traffic. When the three agitated-looking men in Joe Kluber's green truck then appeared out of the driveway at 15035, they saw the U-Haul just a few car lengths in front of them. Witnesses said the trio jumped from the stolen truck—leaving it parked in the middle of traffic—and appeared to run after the U-Haul, hollering *"Hell! Hell!"* or something like that at the rental truck.

It was located a few hours later, abandoned in a parking lot in nearby Northfield, Ohio. It became the starting point for the investigation.

First, recalls Lieutenant Zembala, he found the gas station where the truck had been rented, and then leafed through the station's rental slips looking for some sort of lead. When he came to the signature "M. Durant," a thought occurred to the detective. "I knew a Durant who was a local hoodlum," he says. "I didn't know if it was the same guy, so we did some checking around. We brought his photo out and showed it to the guys at the gas station and they say, 'Oh yeah! This is the same guy. He rented a truck here on many occasions, and he'd always dressed completely in white or completely in black.'

"So," says Zembala, "we've got Durant."

The next clue came from the desk clerk at the nearby Sunset motel. She recounted to local detectives how a strange guest had appeared suddenly that afternoon. The large man, who said his car had broken down, rented a room, made a telephone call and then left in a car with a woman. He had signed in as "M. Pietro."

"We know our hoods around here," says Detective Zembala with a chuckle. "M. Pietro," he explains, was an alias commonly used by Nick Pietroangelo, a familiar face in the Collingwood district. Pietroangelo, according to Zembala, was the man to hire when you needed muscle on a caper.

They checked out the telephone number he dialed from the motel. The phone was listed to a woman in Euclid, Ohio, a Cleveland suburb not far from the Collingwood district. When the police asked this woman if she remembered picking up someone at a motel in Northfield, she answered, "Yeah, I picked up Nick Pietroangelo." She added that Pietroangelo seemed nervous that day, and that he was carrying a gun.

Working now on the solid assumption that the murder was the work of Collingwood hoods, the sheriff's detectives reviewed what they knew of Durant and Pietroangelo's closest associates. Among other possibilities, they thought of Hobart Margroff, a man Lieutenant Zembala describes as very violent, irrational and quick on the trigger when alarmed. They showed Margroff's mug shot to Joe Kluber, who positively identified him.

"So now we've got three guys," remembers Zembala, "and we think there is a fourth [the U-Haul driver]. But we don't have enough to charge anyone. At this point, as long as they kept their mouths shut, there was nothing we could do."

Nothing, indeed, for ten long years. Then a prison snitch, developed through the FBI, told the detectives that the fourth man in the Chapek killing, the U-Haul driver, was named Alan Hilts, who at the time was resident within the Ohio state penal system.

Alan Hilts. *Al!* It hadn't been *"Hell!"* the gang members shouted that afternoon as they ran from Joe Kluber's truck through the stalled traffic on Alexander Road. It had been *"Hey, Al!"*

The police went to visit Al Hilts.

"Fuck you," was one of Hilts's friendlier remarks. "I don't know anything about it. Don't bother me."

Then Zembala's boss, chief of detectives Louis Kulis, and an FBI agent named Tom Kirk paid a second call on Hilts. Their more compelling presentation to the incarcerated Hilts was that time was getting tight. Sooner or later, they said, either he or one of his former pals was going to sing to save his skin, and it might as well be him. If Hilts didn't cooperate, they added, he was looking at the good chance of getting another fifteen years of hard time when the Chapek case came down. Suddenly persuaded, Hilts agreed to testify.

The full story, as provided by Al Hilts and Nick Pietroangelo and then corroborated by a former safecracker Charlie Broeckel (who swore Hobart Margroff had confessed the whole thing to him) was that the gang had surprised Edwin Chapek alone at home, then took him down into the basement and tied him up. Durant, Margroff and Pietroangelo barely had begun to ransack the house in search of Dr. Porbe's coin collection when Al Hilts, at the wheel of the U-Haul, saw Joe Kluber's green truck headed down the drive. Hilts panicked and drove away, leaving his buddies to fend for themselves.

Meanwhile, Edwin Chapek had escaped his ropes and, unwisely, ran upstairs and outside. Hobart Margroff discovered the escape and decided it was time for him to leave too. He jumped into Joe Kluber's green truck and started to drive away, straight toward where Edwin Chapek was hiding in some weeds near the edge of his driveway. At the sight of his friend's vehicle, Chapek popped up to wave and received in return two fatal slugs from Margroff's nine-millimeter handgun. At Margroff's shout ("He's gone!") Durant and Pietroangelo left Joe Kluber on the kitchen floor and ran out to jump in his truck with Margroff, who evidently did not tell them at the time he had just killed Mr. Chapek.

Once a grand jury heard this tale, the Cuyahoga County investigators secured sealed murder indictments against Durant, Margroff and Nick Pietroangelo (who later copped a plea and was sentenced to probation and a fine). But then the police were faced with a choice. Durant, it was believed, was somewhere in the west, perhaps Las Vegas, where he was wanted for robbery and other crimes. Hobart Margroff was in Cleveland. Whichever of the two they went after first, they feared, the other would hear of the arrest and disappear. Since Hobart Margroff was known to have done the actual shooting and was, in any event, a greater danger to public safety than Donald Durant, it was decided to arrest him first. He was later tried and convicted for the Chapek murder, and is serving a life sentence for the crime.

Donald Anthony Durant took it on the lam, as expected. What the Cuyahoga County sheriff's team did not anticipate was that Durant would stay gone for more than eight years. Lieutenant Chester Zembala, for one, is incredulous. "The guy is not competent enough to avoid being caught," he insists. "And his girlfriend's the same way! She was always in trouble, always getting picked up by the police."

Therefore, says Zembala, he believes Donald Durant has met one of the three fates. The first—mentioned jokingly—is that he is now an FBI informer. "If so," says the detective laughingly, "forget about catching him." More seriously, Zembala thinks "he might have died of natural causes and there was no reason to take his fingerprints. In that case, also forget it. Three, he died a violent death because he couldn't be trusted and he's buried in concrete in some freeway underpass somewhere. We may never know."

5. Floater

TEDDY LYNN ELLIS
Cleveland County, Oklahoma

DATE OF BIRTH: AUGUST 1, 1964
HEIGHT: FIVE FEET, EIGHT INCHES
WEIGHT: 140 POUNDS
HAIR: BROWN
EYES: HAZEL
DISTINGUISHING MARKS OR SCARS: TATTOOS ON LEFT AND RIGHT FOREARMS. SCARS ON FOREHEAD, NEAR RIGHT EYE, ON RIGHT ARM, CHEST AND LEFT HAND.
REWARD: UNSPECIFIED AMOUNT
CONTACT: OKLAHOMA STATE DEPARTMENT OF CORRECTIONS ESCAPE TEAM (405) 425-2568, OR 2570

At first it appeared that the Oklahoma State Bureau of Investigation (OSBI) was up against a tough case to crack. In June of 1982 in sparsely settled Pottawatomie County, southeast of Oklahoma City, fishermen discovered a male corpse washed up on a sandbar in the Little River. Fingerprints indicated that the floater was Dale Spurgin, a fugitive from Kansas wanted in a theft case there. Spurgin's autopsy revealed he was a gunshot victim, murdered by a bullet to his chest and another in the head. There was almost nothing else for the OSBI in-

Teddy Lynn Ellis

vestigators to go on except for the strong likelihood that Spurgin had been killed some miles
upstream in neighboring Cleveland County, and
that his lifeless body had drifted westward with
the river's current into Pottawatomie County.

On the chance that someone, somewhere had
information about the crime, the OSBI arranged for the facts of the case to be aired by

the Oklahoma City Police Department's Crime-stopper program, one of the first and most successful in the United States. Sure enough, an anonymous source did phone in. The caller directed the OSBI's attention to seventeen-year-old Teddy Ellis (who already had been in several scrapes with the law), and Ellis's two friends, Johnny Goetz and Andrew Porter, all of tiny Little Axe, Oklahoma, southeast of Oklahoma City. Not long thereafter Goetz and Porter fingered their pal Teddy Ellis as Dale Spurgin's killer.

According to Paul Renfrow, an OSBI public information officer, on the day of the murder in early June 1982, Ellis, Goetz and Porter were out driving around together through hilly and heavily forested Cleveland County. The youths came upon Spurgin, who was hitchhiking. They picked him up and continued driving around, drinking beer and talking. At one point, they stopped the car to do some target shooting with Ellis's .44 pistol.

Spurgin then produced from his backpack a gun of his own, a nifty antique pistol that he showed around with some pride. Teddy Ellis coveted the old gun. Back in the car and driving again, Ellis whispered to one of his friends that he was going to rob Spurgin, and instructed the driver to head for a remote bridge over the Little River, where Teddy intended the robbery to take place.

"They went to the bridge under the pretense of firing this antique pistol down into the river," explains Renfrow. "What we believe happened is that Ellis shot Spurgin once in the chest with this antique, and he didn't fall. It surprised them all. He just kind of stood there with a shocked look on his face. Teddy then produced the other weapon and shot Spurgin in the head and threw his body off the bridge into the water. Then it floated downstream to where it was found in Pottawatomie County."

In September of 1982, Teddy Lynn Ellis pleaded guilty to Spurgin's murder and received a life sentence. Four years later, on the evening of May 24, 1986, at the medium-security Dick Conner Correctional Center in Hominy, Oklahoma, Teddy Ellis and four other inmates escaped. The group crawled through a storm drain under one periphery fence, then cut through a second wire barrier. All except Ellis have been recaptured.

Since 1986, anonymous tipsters have again offered the OSBI information about Teddy Ellis. One person telephoned to say he had moved to California and died there. Another insisted Teddy had joined the navy. Neither lead panned out. "We have nothing substantial about his whereabouts at all," says Renfrow of the OSBI.

6. Colleen's Boyfriend

RICHARD J. CHURCH
Woodstock, Illinois

DATE OF BIRTH: MARCH 24, 1969
HEIGHT: FIVE FEET, ELEVEN INCHES
WEIGHT: 175 POUNDS
HAIR: BROWN
EYES: BLUE
ALSO KNOWN AS: "RICK," RICKIE CHARNEY, RANDY HUNT, RONNIE QUINLEN
REWARD: UNSPECIFIED AMOUNT
CONTACT: HERB PITZMAN
         CHIEF OF POLICE
         WOODSTOCK, ILLINOIS
         (815) 338-2131

Rick Church and Colleen Ritter were sweethearts. Both grew up in solid, respectable middle-class families in Woodstock, Illinois,* a village of 15,000 situated northwest of Chicago, not far from the Wisconsin border. Rick's father, Gene Church, worked for Commonwealth Edison. So did Colleen's dad, Roy Ritter. Both men also served on the local Little League

---

*Woodstock is familiar to fans of the late cartoonist Chester Gould, who selected it as the hometown for his hero, Detective Dick Tracy.

Richard J. Church   *(photos Courtesy Herb Pitzman)*

board. Both families were strongly Catholic. The Churches and the Ritters were good friends.

At Marian Central High School, Rick Church was an all-around athlete. He started at center on the school's state AAA championship football team. Church's coach, Don Penza, would later remember the youth to a Chicago *Tribune* reporter as "very intelligent, a strong-minded boy, but an excellent cooperative student." Colleen Ritter, two years younger than Rick, was a popular and pretty cheerleader. They dated steadily for two and a half years until the summer of 1988. Then, on a Sunday morning in August, the sort of horrifying, inexplicable violence that is supposed to happen elsewhere struck quiet Woodstock, Illinois, and plunged its residents into anguished astonishment.

After the tragedy, Rick's friends told reporters of traits in the boy that in retrospect seemed ominous to them. "He just had a short fuse," recalled a classmate, Mathew Woodruff. "There would be times when he was cool, so good to be around. Then he would turn on you if things didn't go his way. As long as they went his way, he'd be happy."

Others said that was how Rick approached his romance with Colleen.

Jim Garrelts, another friend from high school, told the *Tribune* of a locker-room incident after a basketball game against a rival high school. "We were sharing the dressing room with Round Lake," said Garrelts, "and one of their guys started mouthing off. Rick turned around and knocked him cold with one punch. For someone not very big, Rick sure is strong."

Yet there was nothing in Rick Church's behavior that suggested the possibility of what was to come. He was "a normal kind of guy," recollected a teammate on the Marian High championship eleven. He was "a typical high-school boy," in the opinion of his principal, Thomas Landers. "He never did anything or said anything that would give an indication something like this would happen."

Friends did notice a change in Rick Church in 1987, his senior year at Marian, when his parents split up and filed for divorce. The ensuing autumn, as a freshman at Northern Illinois University in De Kalb, he first began to talk of suicide. According to Mathew Woodruff, who also entered NIU in '87, his old high-school friend started getting into bar fights. Rick's grades, which had been excellent at Marian, deteriorated. He became more possessive toward—and obsessive about—Colleen, going so far as to paper one wall of his dorm room with her photos, including one poster-size picture of her posing as rock star Cyndi Lauper.

Rick Church just barely managed to avoid academic dismissal from NIU that year. He returned home for the summer of 1988 to work as a Little League umpire. He lived with his mother, Cherry, in an apartment she'd rented and saw very little of his friends and neighbors through June and into July.

Then came calamity. Colleen, whom friends say was wearying of Rick's obsessiveness, told him that she felt they should start seeing other people. Her parents had encouraged Colleen to make the break.

Not long afterward, Church and a couple of

his buddies went on an outing to Lake Geneva, in Wisconsin. "He was drinking a lot," Sean Noonan told a reporter. "And when he got drunk, he started shouting about how much he hated women—and especially Colleen for dumping him. He got loud and obnoxious. A girl told him to quiet down and he really went off. We had to hold him back from going after her. All the way home in the car he kept mumbling about Colleen and saying, 'How could she do this to me?'"

According to the *Tribune,* on Saturday night, August 20, Rick Church went to the Ritter house to plead his case once again. He threatened to kill himself if Colleen refused him. She was firm but diplomatic. "Some friends," reported the paper, "thought Colleen had managed to calm Rick down before he left the Ritter house, and she hoped he would accept her decision."

A little after five o'clock the next morning, one of the Ritters' neighbors was awakened by a man shouting "Get out of here!" and then screams of terror coming from the Ritter residence. Moments later, Chris Gehrke, who lived across the street from the Ritters, also heard a scream and looked out his window. He saw a blood-splattered Colleen Ritter running from her front door toward him. A male figure—Rick Church—was sprinting after her. Church caught his estranged girlfriend at the pavement and resumed his assault.

"He was like a maniac," Gehrke remembered, "hitting her until she stopped moving." Just then, as Gerhke recalled, Rick Church looked up and realized someone was watching. Gehrke kept staring as Church ran away around a corner of the Ritters' house.

He had already disappeared when another neighbor, Jim Meisel, ran into the street to Colleen's battered body. Meisel, a onetime rescue-squad member, saw a huge gash wound on the teenager's neck and began to administer first aid. "I didn't know what had happened," he later told reporter Angela Burden of the *Northwest Herald*. "It was a bloody mess. Her hair, face and T-shirt were covered with blood. She was conscious, but did not talk. I just got busy on her serious gash wound and did not take much notice of anything else around me."

Colleen would survive her wounds; her parents were not so fortunate. When the Woodstock paramedic team arrived at the house a few minutes later, they found Mr. and Mrs. Ritter lying close to one another in their living room, savagely beaten and dying. Both had suffered furious blows to the head. Roy Ritter had been stabbed repeatedly with a sharp-pronged instrument, reportedly a trash stick.

Also in the house was Colleen's little brother, Matthew, and a twelve-year-old friend. Matthew told the police that he and his friend had tried to barricade their room with Matthew's bed. Church, however, fought his way in and was about to attack the boys when Colleen Ritter ran screaming from the house. It appears that this desperate act saved both Colleen and the boys from being murdered.

Following his rampage, Rick Church escaped out of town in his mother's 1981 blue Dodge pickup. Despite a massive manhunt mounted throughout the regions west and north of

Woodstock, by midafternoon on Sunday Church had made it 150 miles northwest across the Wisconsin state line to Wisconsin Dells, where he checked into a motel, paying cash. He left the next morning, after appropriating from his room a blanket, some towels, soap and a drinking glass.

A month later, the blue pickup was recovered from a 7-Eleven parking lot in West Hollywood, California. A clerk in the store recognized a photo of Church. Since that time there have been no further leads, although Woodstock police chief Herb Pitzman believes Rick Church probably is still in the southern California area. In January of 1990, a group of local businessmen rented a billboard in West Hollywood. The giant sign bears the young man's likeness and requests that anyone with information come forward.

So far, no one has.

7. The Police Chief

GREGORY JON WEBB
Lyons, Nebraska

DATE OF BIRTH: JULY 23, 1950
HEIGHT: SIX FEET, SIX INCHES
WEIGHT: 215 POUNDS
HAIR: BROWN
EYES: BROWN
OTHER: REDDISH FACIAL HAIR. WAS MUSTACHIOED AT TIME OF DISAPPEARANCE.
REWARD: NEBRASKA CRIMESTOPPERS WILL PAY AN UNSPECIFIED SUM FOR INFORMATION LEADING TO APPREHENSION. (INSIDE NEBRASKA ONLY) CALL (800) 422-1495
CONTACT: NEBRASKA STATE PATROL
    SERGEANT DAN SCOTT
    (402) 471-4545
    OR
    BURT COUNTY SHERIFF'S OFFICE
    (402) 374-2788

Sioux City, Iowa, native Greg Webb was a strapping fellow, well respected around little (population: 1,214) Lyons, Nebraska, where he served as chief of the town's two-man police force. An avid gun collector (including assault weapons) and a would-be soldier of fortune (Webb journeyed to Africa in 1977 and fought

Gregory Jon Webb

as a mercenary in the Rhodesian civil war), he was, according to Lyons mayor Leland Going, "very low-key." As Going told the Lincoln *Star* in early 1987, "[Webb] had no friends in town. That's what made him a good officer. He had no outside pressures. People respected him very much. He was fair."

Perhaps so, but the part about no outside pressures appears to be a misstatement.

Sometime around the middle of 1986, the usually affable Chief Webb began to seem a bit out of phase to some of his associates. The changes in him were for the most part subtle—nothing so apparent, for example, as a facial tic or sudden outbursts of rage—but they were nonetheless noticeable. Most obvious was Webb's new drinking habit. Early-evening callers to his upper-floor duplex apartment in Lyons would often find their normally temperate chief facedown drunk at his table, an empty fifth on the floor beside him.

Because Greg Webb habitually kept things to himself, it was difficult to divine a cause for his emotional unease, if that, indeed, was what it was. Everyone in Lyons knew he was divorced for the second time in the summer of 1986. Not quite everyone also knew that after the divorce Webb began an affair with a townswoman. Hardly anyone, however, knew about Gregg and his downstairs neighbor until he murdered her.

The outline of the case, as provided by Burt County sheriff Leonard Canarsky, is that Greg Webb met thirty-four-year-old Anna Marie Miller Anton through a mutual friend in Iowa. If Webb and Anton were lovers, Canarsky isn't saying, but that seems to be a good guess. It is a matter of record that Mrs. Anton soon moved down from Iowa to Lyons and took the apartment beneath Webb's in the two-unit duplex residence.

Anna Marie was, in Sheriff Canarsky's words, "a hippie and a drinker." She also told whoppers. One of her tall tales was that her husband, Tom, was some big-time drug dealer against whom Anna Marie had once testified in court. She claimed now to live in fear since Tom had vowed to "get" her. These assertions, upon later inspection, proved to be wholly false.

Another story (which could have been true) was that she'd badly hurt her leg in a car wreck. Anna Marie Anton definitely walked with a limp. Also empirically obvious was that she had no money (Mrs. Anton lived on food stamps) and liked to drink. What money she had, or was given, was spent in bars.

Anna Marie was last seen alive on December 15, 1986. Eight days later, Chief Webb personally filled out a missing person's report. Four days after that, on the morning of December 27, Anna Marie's nude body, wrapped in a rug, was found by a farmer in an open field on the Winnebago Indian Reservation about twenty miles north of Lyons in Walhill, Nebraska. She'd been outside, with three .38 slugs in her, for quite some time. Freezes and thaws had ravaged the corpse. Yet the body was unmistakably that of Anna Marie Miller Anton. Chief Greg Webb officially identified her himself.

Leonard Canarsky declines to lay out the full range of reasons why the investigation into Anna Marie's murder was so soon narrowed to Greg Webb. The murder weapon has not been recovered. But a search of her apartment did yield important physical evidence, including blood specimens that connected Webb with the crime.

The sheriff says he did not tip his hand, but it would seem difficult for the chief of police in a town of 1,200 not to know that the county sheriff thinks him a killer. Greg Webb went to work for two more days, then emptied his savings account, traded in his '71 red Mercury

Cougar for a '75 Chevrolet Impala and blew out of town on December 30.

Some days later, the Impala was recovered in a parking lot at Houston's Intercontinental Airport. There, Webb bought a one-way airline ticket to Belize in Central America, and someone—maybe even Webb himself—used the ticket. To this day, that is all that anyone knows, or is willing to admit that they know, about the former police chief of Lyons, Nebraska.

8. The Motive was Money

JOE SINNOTT EDWARDS
Pontiac, Illinois

DATE OF BIRTH: MAY 20, 1964
HEIGHT: FIVE FEET, TEN INCHES
WEIGHT: 165 POUNDS
HAIR: DARK BROWN
EYES: BLUE-GRAY TO HAZEL
DISTINGUISHING MARKS OR SCARS: POSSIBLE SMALL CROSS TATTOO ON LEFT HAND BETWEEN THUMB AND INDEX FINGER
OTHER: DRUG USER, BELIEVED TO BE SUICIDAL
ALSO KNOWN AS: JOSEPH SINNOTT, JOSE SINNOTT, JOSEPH WENZLAFF, JOSEPH WICKAM
REWARD: UP TO $10,000
CONTACT: LIVINGSTON COUNTY SHERIFF'S OFFICE
DETECTIVE JOHN E. JOHNSON
(815) 844-7171
FAX 844-5774, EXT. 140

Who murdered Rob and Marcia Edwards? The local authorities think it was their adopted son, Joe, together with an accomplice.

Why would Joe want Rob and Marcia dead? Well, in the Edwardses' kitchen police investigators found a hand-lettered note, possibly in Mrs. Edwards's hand. It reads in its entirety: "Joe and friend made abusive threats want money if . . ." After "if" the pen line trails dis-

**Joe Sinnott Edwards in 1978, and in a sketch
of how he might appear today**
*(photo and sketch courtesy: John E. Johnson,
Livingston County Sheriff's Office)*

tractedly off the page. Little else is known about
the direct causes or circumstances of one of
the most baffling homicide cases in the history
Livingston County, Illinois.

The strange tale begins in 1970 when Rob Edwards, then thirty-five, met and married thirty-
three-year-old Marcia. They started their life
together in a house about a mile outside of Pontiac, Illinois, which lies along the Vermilion
River in Livingston County, southwest of Chicago.

Rob was a graduate of the University of Illinois and served as a Green Beret in Vietnam.
In Pontiac, he worked for a local building contractor, stayed active in the army reserve and
joined the Pontiac Elks Club, of which he became an Exalted Ruler. Edwards also belonged
to the Pontiac Area Planning Commission. Marcia, a former public-school gym coach in Chi-

cago, joined several Pontiac-area service clubs and organizations, including the Pontiac Women's Club, where she served a term as president.

The Edwardses were unable to conceive a child, but they wanted a family. So they consulted a central Illinois adoption agency that put the couple in touch with the Salem Children's Home in Flannigan, Illinois, about ten miles south of Pontiac. It was at the Salem orphanage in 1977 that they found and adopted thirteen-year-old Joe Sinnott.

Records indicate that Joe was born in Chicago and then, at a very early age, was abandoned by his mother to the care of a baby-sitter. Over the coming years he was shunted in and out of several foster households in the Chicago area before being sent south to live with a family in Bloomington, Illinois, not far from Flannigan. According to Livingston County sheriff's detective John E. Johnson, Joe started getting into "significant mischief" in Bloomington, which resulted in his removal to the Salem Children's Home.

His behavior problems only worsened in Pontiac, where Joe Sinnott Edwards proved to be a constant discipline problem at the local high school. His police rap sheet included a charge that he vandalized a house under construction. At home, he was hostile toward his new parents; police records show that Joe physically menaced the Edwardses. He began to drink liquor and to sniff glue and made several serious attempts at suicide, both by slitting his wrists and taking drug overdoses that required hospitalization.

After just two years, the embattled Edwardses gave up. On March 9, 1979, Rob Edwards rewrote his will to exclude his adopted son: "I have purposely omitted my son from this will for personal reasons," he wrote. Three months later, on June 14, Marcia Edwards also altered her will. "At the time of making this will I am not unmindful of my son, Joe Edwards," read the new document. "I have not made provision for him in my new will, not from lack of affection, but because his circumstances are presently such that he is not in a position to accept financial responsibilities."

Indeed. Fifteen-year-old Joe, in the aftermath of his house-wrecking episode, had just been ordered placed in a "controlled situation"—i.e., a reform school. But Rob and Marcia Edwards had not totally abandoned their adopted son. With the court's approval, they paid for him to be sent to a private facility, the North Dakota Boys Ranch near Minot, North Dakota, where, it was hoped, he would straighten himself out.

He didn't.

Joe Edwards tried many times to run away from the North Dakota Boys Ranch, once stealing a car as part of his escape attempt. He was entirely intractable, an incorrigible, and was returned to his parents' custody in October of 1980. Joe did not reenter Pontiac High. Instead (as far as the police can determine) he left town soon after Rob and Marcia brought him home from North Dakota.

The Edwardses may have believed Joe's next destination was a trade school in Florida. All that is known for sure is that he next turned up in Ann Arbor, Michigan, where he had acquired a nine-millimeter handgun. Witnesses also recounted how Joe Edwards talked of wanting to kill his adoptive parents. Apparently, he stayed in Ann Arbor until the summer of 1981 when he vanished completely.

Eighteen months later, on Friday morning, January 21, 1983, Rob Edwards failed to show up for work. Since Edwards was always a punctual employee, Rob's boss at the contracting company soon began to worry. He tried calling Edwards at home. No answer. He tried raising Rob via the mobile phone in his company-issued Bronco. Nothing.

Alarmed, the boss then drove out to the Edwards house. All the doors were locked. Around back, however, he could peer through the sliding glass doors of the Edwardses' combination TV and rec room. There, on the floor near the kitchen, lay Marcia Edwards, murdered. She had taken two nine-millimeter slugs in the face. The Edwards family dog, a middle-sized mutt of indeterminate genetic heritage, stood guard in the pool of blood surrounding her. When the police arrived, they were forced to employ a long pole with a noose to pull the snarling animal away from his dead mistress.

Marcia's husband, also dead, was discovered in the front seat of their 1979 Lincoln, which was parked in a narrow alleyway not far from the house. Rob was nearly prone on the seat, with two nine-millimeter slugs in the back of his head. The bullets had been fired by the same weapon used to kill Mrs. Edwards.

The Livingston County Sheriff's Office is reluctant to discuss how it came to believe that Joe Edwards—and perhaps an accomplice—killed his parents. It is a matter of public record, though, that the investigation went on until

August of 1984 before Joe was charged in the homicide.

There was the incriminating note found in the kitchen. Also, a witness placed Joe in Pontiac on the eighteenth. Another person thought he saw Joe and a companion in a green pickup truck in town on the twentieth. A neighbor reported seeing a similar-sounding vehicle parked in the Edwardses' long driveway. This witness further recollected noting the Edwardses' Lincoln parked in their utility shed about ten o'clock the night before the crime. Two people were sitting in the car, but it is not known if either was positively identified.

Complicating the investigation and the hunt for Joe Edwards is the fact that no official records of his fingerprints exists. Joe was never booked for a crime in Illinois, and North Dakota (where he stole the car) neither photographs nor fingerprints juveniles. The only similar identifying print, Joe's foot impressions taken at birth in a Chicago hospital, were lost in a fire. Likewise, Joe has a social security number but has never used it.

Joe Edwards has been on the run for more than seven years now, a long time for a young man to be lost in America. Whether he feels remorse for his alleged crimes is, of course, unknown. But if, as the handwritten note found in the Edwardses' kitchen suggests, his motive that January night was money, then Joe certainly may ponder how he would have fared had he been able to curb his hostility and self-destructiveness. In 1987, four years after they were murdered, a court approved disbursal of the bulk of the Edwardses' state to two beneficiaries, the Elks Club and Rob's old fraternity at the University of Illinois. The amount, which at one time probably would have gone to Joe alone, came to $800,000.

9. An Ordinary Man

WILLIAM THOMAS SMITH
Minnetonka, Minnesota

DATE OF BIRTH: OCTOBER 15, 1924
HEIGHT: FIVE FEET, FOUR INCHES
WEIGHT: 140 POUNDS
HAIR: GRAY
EYES: BLUE
ALSO KNOWN AS: WILLY
REWARD: $1,000
CONTACT: MINNETONKA, MINNESOTA, POLICE DEPARTMENT
CORPORAL WALTER COUDRON
(612) 933-1604
OR
CRIMESTOPPERS
(612) 45-CRIME

Diminutive Willy Smith, formerly of Minnetonka, Minnesota, near Minneapolis, is in most ways just an ordinary person with an ordinary name. A vacuum-cleaner repairman by trade, Smith enjoys playing bridge and square dancing. As far as the police know, he has never been issued a traffic ticket.

Every now and then, however, something sets Willy off. Back in the 1950s, in his home state of Ohio, he was charged with a violent sex of-

William Thomas Smith *(photo: courtesy F.B.I.)*

fense. Then there was the bizarre and deadly
first week of January 1977.

On Monday, January 3, the first workday of
the new year, Smith asked his boss at the vacuum dealership in Minnetonka if he could have
a couple weeks' vacation. He explained that he
needed time to work on patching up his relationship with his former wife, forty-four-year-

old Joan Vera Fields. At the time, she was seeing another man, Robert Zempel, of Brooklyn Park, a suburb north of Minneapolis.

That evening at about six o'clock Joan Fields was at Zempel's residence when Willy Smith drove up in his red 1971 Chevy Vega. According to Zempel's later affidavit, he was on the telephone when Smith walked in, brandishing a nickel-plated .32.

"I'll give you to the count of three to get off the phone," Willy announced. Then he herded the startled Zempel and Ms. Fields into the living room, where he instructed the couple to sit together on a small chair.

Robert Zempel was more irritated than scared.

"I'm the ex-husband!" said Smith in a tone Zempel found laughably self-important.

"So big deal, you're the ex-husband," his prisoner replied.

Ignoring the sarcasm, Willy Smith told Zempel that he was going to lock him in a closet for the next four or five hours while he and Joan discussed their future. "If she decides to stay with you," he explained, "she can come back and let you out."

Willy locked his rival in the closet and barricaded its door with pieces of furniture. Then he drove Joan down to Minnetonka, where they checked into the Knoll-Way Motel as Mr. and Mrs. William Smith. They were given Unit 2, which rented for $14.56 a night. Shortly past ten o'clock, Joan called a relative from Unit 2 to see if he could come pick her up and take her back to Zempel's. She did not appear upset or frightened, but she also did not call back. Meantime, Robert Zempel extricated himself from his prison. He thought about calling the police, but decided to wait until the next day, January 4.

The management at the Knoll-Way had nothing unusual to report about Mr. and Mrs. Smith in Unit 2. One clerk remembered that they came to the front desk on the fourth, asking for a newspaper. That night, however, Willy Smith showed up at a friend's house in Minnetonka. He was alone and very drunk. Smith said nothing except to ask for a place to sleep. On the morning of the fifth he was gone before daybreak.

Later that morning, the day manager at the Knoll-Way walked by Unit 2 and noticed that a light was on inside. Smith's red Vega was missing. She peeked into the room to see a figure under the covers of the bed. It was Joan Vera Fields and she appeared to be sleeping. At one o'clock that afternoon, the manager returned and saw that Mrs. Smith had not stirred. The reason, immediately evident when the manager pulled down the covers, was that Joan Fields was dead from a gunshot wound to the chest.

The next day, Thursday, January 6, Willy Smith's Vega was recovered one block away from the bus station in Des Moines, Iowa, about a three-and-a-half-hour drive south from Minnetonka. There was a parking ticket on the windshield. Inside, police found some magazines, an audiocassette tape labeled *Jammin' with the Who and the Rolling Stones* and a partially empty bottle of vodka. Smith was a heavy smoker. The auto's ashtray was crammed with dead butts.

Since then, Smith has twice been reported in Texas—once in the east Texas town of Tyler, and again, in 1984, at a shopping mall in Irving, which is between Dallas and Fort Worth. In the second instance, the person who saw him was a former neighbor who was surprised to see his old acquaintance turn and run in unfeigned fright when their eyes met.

That is as close as the Minnetonka cops have come to finding Willy Smith. Thirteen years after Joan Fields's murder, they are not at all optimistic that they will ever catch him. He's just too ordinary, too lacking in distinctiveness to give himself away, unless, as has happened before, something once again sets Willy Smith off.

10. "Buried in the Streets"

MAURICE HERMAN MACK
Southfield, Michigan

DATE OF BIRTH: NOVEMBER 15, 1971
HEIGHT: FIVE FEET, SEVEN INCHES
WEIGHT: 150 POUNDS
HAIR: BLACK
EYES: BROWN
REWARD: THE STATE OF MICHIGAN WILL PAY AN UNSPECIFIED SUM FOR INFORMATION LEADING TO MAURICE MACK'S ARREST.
CONTACT: MICHIGAN STATE POLICE
      FUGITIVE TEAM
      (313) 525-2560
      OR
      SOUTHFIELD POLICE DEPARTMENT
      DETECTIVE TED QUISENBERRY
      (313) 354-4750

Maurice Mack's mother dealt drugs and was murdered several years ago in the course of her work. The Southfield, Michigan, police believe that Maurice's father is still alive, but they don't know where he is. According to their information, Maurice has long been a street kid who

113

Maurice Herman Mack

sometimes stayed at his uncle's house in South-field, when his uncle was out of jail.

Unsurprisingly, Maurice Mack left school at an early age to join the drug trade, specializing in a particularly speculative and dangerous end of the business. He and his buddy Monte Matthews, detectives say, ripped off drug dealers. Maurice and Monte would pose as drug wholesalers, then rob the dealers when they showed up to purchase their product.

This, apparently, was the planned scenario on the night of January 28, 1989, when Detroit drug dealer LaDonne Johnson, twenty-eight, drove his 1988 red Mercury Cougar out to Southfield, expecting to buy $30,000 worth of cocaine from Mack and Matthews, who awaited Johnson at Mack's uncle's house.

The partners had dummied up a couple sacks of white powder. Johnson, according to the story later told by Monte Matthews, wanted to test the substance. Still according to Matthews, before the dealer could discover the scam, Maurice nearly blew Johnson's head off.

Two days later, responding to telephone tips, the Southfield police searched the house and discovered drug gear, as well as blood and bits of bone and brain tissue. The next day, January 31, the rest of LaDonne Johnson, clad in his acid-washed jeans, black and red FILA jacket and white hightops, was found in the trunk of his red Cougar in a Southfield parking lot.

Monte Matthews was picked up by the Detroit police. On February 15, he was arraigned for his role in the killing. He was tried and convicted in the summer of 1989. At trial, Matthews testified that Maurice Mack was the shooter.

Mack, who is a member of one or more street gangs, and is said to travel on drug business back and forth between Detroit and New York City, has been seen several times by informants, but has not yet been captured by the authorities. "He's a slippery guy," says Southfield homicide detective Ted Quisenberry. "He knows how to keep himself in hiding. Mack's buried in the streets somewhere."

11. "A Beaut"

HENRIETTA MARIA GANOTE
Lincoln, Nebraska

DATE OF BIRTH: SOMETIME IN 1962
HEIGHT: FIVE FEET, SEVEN INCHES
WEIGHT: 139 POUNDS
HAIR: BROWN
EYES: BROWN
DISTINGUISHING MARKS OR SCARS: TATTOOS ON BOTH
  THIGHS, RIGHT WRIST AND RIGHT SHOULDER
REWARD: NEBRASKA CRIMESTOPPERS WILL PAY AN UNSPE-
  CIFIED AMOUNT FOR INFORMATION LEADING TO GANOTE'S
  APPREHENSION. CALL (INSIDE NEBRASKA ONLY)
  (800) 422-1495
CONTACT: NEBRASKA STATE PATROL
         SERGEANT DAN SCOTT
         (402) 471-4545

Early on the morning of September 8, 1980, a
Lancaster County, Nebraska, deputy sheriff responded to a 911 call at an apartment complex
on the south side of Lincoln, the county seat.
He was shown into a shabby, three-room upstairs unit by Henrietta Ganote, eighteen, whom
the deputy would later describe as "eerily
calm." When he asked Ganote what her trouble
was, she directed his attention to her sixteen-
month-old daughter, Jessie, who lay still and

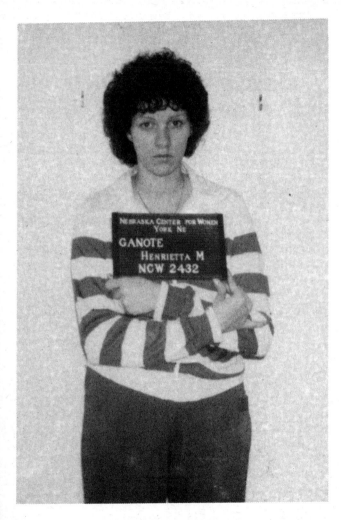

Henrietta Maria Ganote

crumpled in her crib. Subsequent examination would show that the child had been bludgeoned to death, probably with a large stone ashtray found in the apartment.

Later on that day, when sheriff's detective Merl Hesser first interrogated Henrietta Ganote, the young mother very coldly explained that her dead baby in the crib, covered with hideous bruises and still wearing a weeks-old cast on her broken leg, had taken a fall down the stairs. Deputy Hesser knew enough about injuries and child abuse to be skeptical.

Then Henrietta said she believed something heavy had fallen on her child, and that was what had killed Jessie. "She was a beaut," says Hesser. Her last story was that her boyfriend, Brad Hess,* had abused the child, an allegation the police took seriously until they questioned Hess at length and heard from him about Henrietta's past behavior with Jessie, tales of broken bones and beatings that a local doctor was able to confirm.

An indictment was sworn out, but Henrietta's trial was delayed because in the course of investigating her, Lincoln law enforcement officials discovered that she had skipped out on an undisclosed conviction in St. Joseph, Missouri, where authorities desired her return. So, while awaiting trial in Nebraska for killing her little girl, Henrietta Ganote served a couple years in the Buckingham County, Missouri, jail—where she once again conceived a child, and not with Mr. Hess.

In June of 1982, several members of her fam-

*a pseudonym

ily came to Lincoln to testify about Henrietta. Some told the judge she was a sweet girl, incapable of harming her baby. Others said she had a history of abusing the child and, no surprise, had been abused as a child herself. In the end, Henrietta waived a jury trial and pleaded no contest to the manslaughter charge. She was sentenced to six to eight years at the minimum-security Nebraska Women's Center near the town of York.

Two years later, Ganote and another inmate burrowed under a fence at the prison and disappeared together into the surrounding cornfields. Since then, there have been reported sightings of Henrietta Ganote in Missouri too. According to these reports, she is now working as an exotic dancer.

SECTION THREE

NORTHEAST

1. Time to Go?

NORMAN ARTHUR PORTER, JR.
Saugus, Massachusetts

DATE OF BIRTH: JANUARY 28, 1940
HEIGHT: FIVE FEET, TEN INCHES
WEIGHT: 160 POUNDS
HAIR: BLOND-GOING-TO-GRAY
EYES: BLUE
DISTINGUISHING MARKS OR SCARS: SCAR ON UPPER LIP HIDDEN BY MUSTACHE WORN AT TIME OF ESCAPE
OTHER: PARTIAL UPPER DENTURE
ALSO KNOW AS: PHILLIP DECHENE
REWARD: NONE
CONTACT: MASSACHUSETTS DEPARTMENT OF CORRECTION
FUGITIVE APPREHENSION UNIT
(617) 727-2181

What is the appropriate punishment for calculated, cold-blooded murder? Is it possible for such a killer to reform and to rejoin society? If so, how does the state determine if, or when, rehabilitation has been achieved? And what about a victim's survivors' demands for retribution?

These are controversial questions everywhere in the United States, difficult to answer and certain to divide any community into adamantly opposing sides. Nowhere, however, have such incendiary—or important—issues been

123

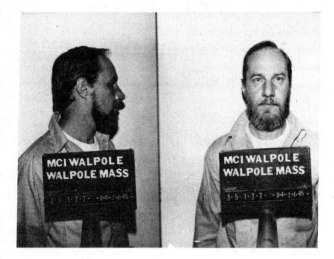

Norman Arthur Porter, Jr.

cast in bolder relief than they have in the case of Norman A. Porter, a fugitive from justice in the commonwealth of Massachusetts.

Massachusetts, of course, also produced the infamous Willie Horton, the imprudently furloughed convict who took advantage of his release to attack a Maryland couple in their house. Horton tied up the husband and cut him with a knife. He also repeatedly raped the man's wife. This crime is usually cited as one of the prime reasons why George Bush, and not former Massachusetts governor Michael Dukakis, became president in 1988.

Controversial as Horton's case became, however, to free him obviously was a dreadful error. The issues in Norman Porter's case were much less clear cut.

There was no suggestion in Porter's early days of crime that he would turn out to be anything more than a common career criminal with a particularly violent nature. He dropped out of school in the eighth grade, subsequently was committed to a series of reform schools and stood accused of three armed robberies in Boston's North Shore area by the time he was twenty years old.

In fact, Norman was awaiting trial for these felonies on Thursday, September 29, 1960, when he and two accomplices attempted to rob a Robert Hall clothing store in Saugus, another North Shore community not far from Lynn, Massachusetts. According to the police account of the stickup, Porter and one of his two cronies forced the store's employees and customers into a back room and then demanded all their money and jewelry. John J. Pigott, a part-time clerk, was reaching into his pocket for his cash when Porter, with no known provocation, placed his shotgun's muzzle against the back of his head and pulled the trigger. "It was more or less an execution," says Captain Curtis M. Wood, commander of the Massachusetts Department of Corrections' Fugitive Apprehension Unit.

Porter was captured and put into the Middlesex County jail. He remained in custody until noon on Sunday, May 14, 1961—Mother's Day—when he and an accused kidnapper, thief and cop killer named Edgar Cook busted out. In the course of their escape (according to Porter's later indictment) Norman physically assaulted David S. Robinson, the master and keeper of the Middlesex jail. Edgar Cook then shot Robinson to death.

The ensuing drama is described in a colorful, if perhaps fanciful, account published in the May 22, 1961, Boston *Evening American.* Porter and Cook split up at once. Two days after the murder, on the evening of Tuesday the sixteenth, the police traced Edgar Cook to a Back Bay apartment, where, as the official version has it, he chose suicide over recapture.

"An ironic twist," reported the *Evening American,* "placed Cook and Porter a short distance apart the night police cornered Cook. . . . In the violent minutes that peaked in Cook's suicide, Porter was trysting on a secluded Back Bay street with a girl he'd met in the Hub theatrical district. As Cook put a gun to his forehead and blew out his brains, Porter was romancing in the back seat of a stolen car."

Still according to the newspaper, Porter roamed through four states in stolen cars in the seven days he remained at large. He was finally captured late at night in Keene, New Hampshire, as he was robbing a food store. Norman had removed to his stolen vehicle about fifty dollars in cash from the register, some canned meat, assorted vegetables, bread, shaving cream and five six-packs of beer. He was just going back for a sixth carton when the Keene police arrived to arrest him.

"Porter cursed himself for going back for more beer," said the *Evening American.* " 'If I hadn't been so greedy I would have been long gone,' he said."

That autumn, Norman Porter pleaded guilty to David Robinson's murder and was sentenced to a life term. He would be eligible for parole in fifteen years. He received the same sentence—to be served consecutively—for the shotgun slaying of John Pigott. Lastly, he was given two life sentences for armed robbery. These were to be served concurrently with the murder terms.

Looking at that much hard time, Norman Porter might have surrendered his spirit, as well as his person, to the grim monotony of prison life. Many convicts facing so many years in the joint simply forget that they ever had any goals or ambitions except to survive. Or they consume themselves with escape schemes.

But Norman Porter was a surprise. Ill lettered as he was, he began to read. Reading led to intellectual curiosity—an entirely novel impulse for Porter—and then to a thirst for higher education. In time, at the maximum-security facility at Walpole, he entered an experimental university program for convicts and ultimately was awarded an undergraduate degree from Boston University.

He wrote poetry, started a prison newspaper and a prison radio station, called Radio Free Norfolk, for the facility where he was being housed at the time. Norman also began to make contacts within Massachusetts's large population of progressive and reform-minded citizens, who, after the deadly 1971 uprising at the Attica Prison in New York where ten guards and thirty-two inmates were killed, began to press for positive changes in their own state's penal system. "Norman befriended them," explains Captain Wood of the Fugitive Apprehension Unit. "He was well liked and he cultivated these people."

By 1975, Porter had gained such recognition

and approval that his first sentence (for the Robinson murder) was commuted and he began to serve his second one, for killing John Pigott. Some people—including Porter himself—believed that he had served enough time and that he should be released altogether.

Typical of his more fervent admirers was a physician, Dr. Alfred DeMaria of Boston. In 1984, the doctor told reporter Adam Gaffin of the Middlesex *News* that "everyone agrees with the facts—that he has been in jail for 23 years, that he has made a remarkable rehabilitation of himself, but he's still in jail." DeMaria, who was working for Porter's immediate release, told the newspaper that he knew of at least 100 telegrams that had been sent to Governor Dukakis in support of Norman's release.

A contrasting view of Porter is offered by Captain Curtis Wood. "I'm speaking as someone from law enforcement," he says. "I'm not qualified to get inside his head or anything. But I know him personally and I've always known him to be a snake in the grass. He has a large ego. He thinks he's a lot more intelligent than other people. And he's extremely arrogant. Always working the angles. He was always skirting the rules, taking advantage, being given breaks."

One such "break," as Wood explains, was Norman's occasional daytime furloughs to Boston, where he'd come from whatever facility he was in for conversation and lunch with the deputy state corrections commissioner. Sometimes, Captain Wood continues, Porter would push too far. He was returned to walled prisons from minimal-security lockups three times. On one occasion he was accused of drug trafficking. Another time, says Wood, "he was caught having illicit sex with a couple [of female] staff members."

The year 1985 found Norman Porter at the Norfolk Prerelease center southwest of Boston, near Walpole. "The superintendent there basically didn't take any grief," explains Wood. "It was a very structured environment. Norman couldn't do what he wanted. He had to check with his supervisor if he wanted to go here or to go there. He started to become a management problem. Basically, he felt that he had done enough time, and he was going to leave. And that is what he did."

Sometime late on the afternoon of December 23, 1985, Norman Porter walked away from the Norfolk facility. He was last seen talking on a pay phone there at 4:30 P.M.

The escape, like his many years of incarceration, sparked public controversy. "I fully support Porter's escape," read a letter written by an acquaintance to the editor of the Middlesex *News.* "When one is confronted with a hypocritical and corrupt system, the only sane, just thing to do is to run from it. I will be pleased if there is anything I can do to keep Porter out of the clutches of 'justice' and to at last be free."

Doris Evans, the late John Pigott's cousin, sharply disagreed with this point of view. "I told you he wasn't ready," she said to a Boston *Globe* reporter. "I told you he wasn't rehabilitated. He has broken another law."

Five years later, Porter is still loose. Captain Wood thinks that Norman may have been helped by some of his supporters. There are indications that Porter may have made his way to Australia. "It wouldn't surprise me if Norman was living somewhere, working at a college," says Wood. "He can impress people like that."

On the other hand, says Wood, the old Norman might resurface too. "I've been in fugitive work for sixteen years," he explains, "and it is rare for someone on the run to start a brand-new life. It happens, but it is rare. More usually they fall back into doing what they did before they were arrested."

2. Sudden Death

SAMUEL J. HUSTON
Lockport, New York

DATE OF BIRTH: DECEMBER 18, 1942
HEIGHT: SIX FEET, TWO INCHES
WEIGHT: 200 POUNDS
HAIR: BLACK
EYES: BROWN
ALSO KNOWN AS: JOSHUA HUSTON
REWARD: THE NEW YORK STATE POLICE WILL PAY AN UN-SPECIFIED AMOUNT FOR INFORMATION LEADING TO HUS-TON'S ARREST
CONTACT: NEW YORK STATE POLICE
(800) 262-4321
OR,
LOCKPORT, NEW YORK, POLICE
(716) 433-7700

Sam and Mary Huston of Lockport, New York, did not have a model marriage—or rather, marriages. They were wed, divorced, wed again and fought all the time, according to their neighbors on Washburn Street in Lockport, a small snowbelt community not far from Niagara Falls. But for all the yelling, slammed doors and broken crockery over the years, no serious Huston household violence had ever been reported

131

Sam J. Huston

to the Lockport police. None, that is, until the night of April 14, 1982.

The Hustons had separated again that spring. Sam, who was then thirty-nine and worked as a laborer, was living with his brother Frank (one of his twelve siblings) about a block away from the Washburn Street residence. Mary, thirty-six, had hired a divorce attorney. She was in the process of moving out of their large, two-story house with her three children, all born to her by two other husbands. She and Sam did not have any children together.

According to what he later told the police, Sam had been in the city of Niagara Falls early on April 14 and had returned to his brother's residence on Evans Street in Lockport that afternoon. He was alone there (Frank had gone fishing) when a process server came to the door with divorce papers from Mary.

Sam admitted under later police questioning that he took the papers and headed, on foot, for the house on Washburn Street, where Mary and her mother, Alison Brown, sixty-seven, were busy with the work of moving. He wanted to discuss the divorce with his estranged wife, he explained. On his way, said Huston, he met a friend of the family, who, coincidentally, was also headed for the Washburn Street address; the friend wanted to look over some of the family furniture Mary had put up for sale. When the two men appeared at the door together, Mrs. Huston admitted the furniture shopper and told her husband she'd talk to him later. This was about 6:30 P.M.

Sometime within the next hour one of Mary's aunts telephoned the house and spoke to Mrs. Brown. She arranged to come by and see her sister in a few minutes. When the aunt arrived, however, she discovered the house was locked up tight and no one would come to the door, even though all the lights were on.

Then, about 10:15 that night, Mary's son Peter, age nine, returned home from the movies to find the house still locked and all the lights still burning. When he couldn't find a way inside, he walked down the street to a Jiffy Mart convenience store and called the police.

The arrival of the cops at the well-lit but eerily silent Huston house soon attracted a crowd. As neighbors and some of Peter's friends looked on, the police tried the doors and then attempted to peek through the windows, which Mary and her mother had covered with newspapers after taking the curtains down. The two women had done a careful job, leaving only one small slit in a kitchen pane. A patrolman went to the single available peephole and gazed through it. Inside, he spotted a female figure lying motionless on the kitchen floor. It was Alison Brown.

The police quickly broke down the backdoor. They found Mrs. Brown on her back, fully clothed and quite dead from a dozen stab wounds to her chest, abdomen and arms. There were defensive wounds on her hands; Alison Brown had tried to ward off her murderer.

Her daughter, by contrast, was apparently taken completely by surprise. Mary Huston, also clothed, was discovered by the police in a small downstairs bathroom, dead from nine stab wounds to her chest and abdomen.

According to a doctor's best estimate, the two women were probably killed between 7:30 and 8:30 that evening. No murder weapon was found, but forensic specialists were able to infer from the victims' wounds that they had both been attacked with a heavy-bladed instrument, about six inches long. There was no sign of a forced entry or evidence of burglary as a motive for the two slayings.

These factors and his marital history made

Samuel J. Huston a prime suspect in the murders of his wife and mother-in-law. In fact, he would be the only suspect in the case. Detectives went to his brother Frank's house and arrested Sam within the hour. His Miranda rights were read to him at the station house at 11:20 that night, and then he was questioned until after five o'clock the next morning.

Huston, who didn't appear to be intoxicated or under the influence of drugs that night, did not avail himself of a lawyer during his interrogation. He had no verifiable alibi, especially for the critical hour between 7:30 and 8:30. But he also admitted to nothing. Detective Captain Henry Newman, one of six detectives who conducted the questioning, remembers that Sam showed no appropriate grief, remorse or anger at his wife and mother-in-law's brutal deaths. "I'd describe him as uncooperative," says Newman.

Later that morning, the district attorney informed the police that they could no longer hold Huston without charging him. Since there were no witnesses to the crime, and no physical evidence implicating Sam save for some unidentified blood on his shoes, he was allowed to go free.

He immediately traveled southwest to Niagara Falls and committed himself to the Memorial Medical Center's mental-health facility there. Whether Huston feared he was unbalanced, or perhaps wanted to lay a foundation for some sort of insanity plea, is unknown. So far, the record of his stay at the center, and any treatment he might have received, is confidential.

The Lockport police did conduct another interrogation of Sam Huston, and once again got nowhere with their suspect. That is about the same direction their investigation took too. Throughout the balance of 1982 and most of 1983 they turned up nothing significant. Sam seemed to gain in confidence as time went by.

Then came a break. A female witness, long reluctant to get involved in the case, at last agreed to tell a grand jury what she knew—that she had overheard Huston confess the killings to a member of his family, including details of how he accomplished the crimes.

The grand jury heard this witness's testimony in November 1983. The panel handed up two second-degree-murder indictments against Huston on January 4, 1984. By then, however, Sam had disappeared. A few weeks later, he became a charter member of the New York State Police's "Twelve Most Wanted List," known familiarly as New York's "Dirty Dozen." Since that time, a total of forty-two fugitives have been placed on the list. Thirty have been returned to justice. But not Sam Huston. Not yet.

3. Savage

ROBERT THOMAS NAUSS, JR.
Philadelphia, Pennsylvania

DATE OF BIRTH: MAY 10, 1952
HEIGHT: FIVE FEET, NINE INCHES
WEIGHT: 190 POUNDS
HAIR: BROWN
EYES: BROWN
DISTINGUISHING MARK OR SCARS: PARROT TATTOO ON UP-
   PER RIGHT ARM; THREE SKULLS ON RIGHT FOREARM. AN-
   OTHER SKULL TATTOO WITH DAGGER AND ''BORN TO
   LOSE'' ON UPPER LEFT ARM. ON LEFT FOREARM A SWAS-
   TIKA AND FEMALE FIGURE.
OTHER: NAUSS IS SENSITIVE ABOUT HIS HEIGHT AND OFTEN
   WEARS BOOTS OR SHOES WITH HIGH HEELS.
ALSO KNOWN AS: ''MATTRESS'' OR ''MUMFORD''
REWARD: UNSPECIFIED AMOUNT FROM PENNSYLVANIA CRIME
   STOPPERS AT 1-800-4-PA-TIPS
CONTACT: PENNSYLVANIA STATE POLICE
            FUGITIVE UNIT
            (215) 581-3144
            OR
            THE U.S. MARSHALS SERVICE
            SUPERVISORY DEPUTY STEPHEN QUINN
            (215) 597-3895

If there is such a phenomenon as a "bad seed,"
a person programmed from birth to eventually

Robert Thomas Nauss, Jr.
(Top right: Bust by Frank Bender, courtesy of FBI)

do evil no matter how positive his or her home environment may be, then Robert Nauss could qualify as an exemplar of the type. He was raised in an upper-middle-class Philadelphia suburb by stable parents whose other children turned out very well. Robert's father owned a successful automobile repair garage, and for some years Robert Nauss *père* assumed that mechanically inclined Robert Nauss *fils* would one day take over the family business.

But young Robert, who like his siblings was educated in strict parochial schools, seemed attracted to the sinister and the violent. According to U.S. marshals who are familiar with his case, this tendency was first noticed in his senior year of high school. Soon after, Nauss's descent into savagery accelerated. While still a teenager, Robert would commit the lowest, most depraved acts imaginable.

His principal association after high school was with the Warlock motorcycle gang, of which he became vice-president. The Warlocks, in the early 1970s, were 250 strong in the Philadelphia area, second only in strength to the Pagans, of whom there were an estimated 450. Both groups, who from time to time warred with one another, were well known among law enforcement officials for the perversions they practiced and for the peril they posed to the rest of the community. The gangs were deeply involved in the manufacture of illegal drugs, especially amphetamines. As part of gang ritual, individual members were expected to offer their girlfriends to the rest of the group for gang raping. Other times, the Warlocks or Pagans would cruise on their Harley-Davidsons, looking for any single girl to kidnap and rape and, allegedly, sometimes murder for fun.

This was Robert Nauss's element. He and six other Warlocks were once convicted of trafficking in methamphetamines. In another case, Nauss was convicted of abducting, raping and assaulting a twenty-two-year-old woman. The victim testified against Nauss, telling the court he held her for two days and forced her to commit various sex acts with him and three other men. Nauss punched her in the stomach, she said, and forced her to drink barbiturate-laced wine.

In 1975, Nauss fathered a son by a fifteen-year-old girl whose heavy drug habit later led to her institutionalization. She had begun hallucinating that she was Snow White.

The crime for which Robert Nauss would be sentenced to serve a life sentence occurred in 1971. At that time he was dating a pretty former beauty pageant winner, twenty-one-year-old Elizabeth Ann Lande, known as "Liz." Petite (just five feet tall), with green eyes and flowing blond hair, Liz had ambitions of becoming an actress. But she also was psychologically afflicted.

"We took her to the best psychiatrists in the city," her father, Frank Lande, would later tell reporter Mike Mallowe for *Philadelphia* magazine. "But she just kept withdrawing. . . . She was even in the hospital for treatment for a while, but they just couldn't seem to help her."

Liz Lande was diagnosed as a schizophrenic, a cause of heartbreak to those, such as her parents, who loved her, but of little apparent consequence to Robert Nauss, who submitted Liz to his buddies for gang rape—twice. She developed a deranged dependence on Nauss, but also fought to free herself from his control. Her father would remember angry telephone calls and nights of motorcycles circling the family house. One time, a bullet whizzed into the rafters. Still, Liz resisted Nauss's attempts to see her.

On December 11, 1971, however, Mr. and Mrs. Lande left for a sea-cruise vacation. Liz assured them she would be okay by herself at home. A short while after the Landes left, however, she was seen getting into a vehicle with a young man answering to Robert Nauss's description.

The rest of the story emerged eight years later at Nauss's trial for Liz's murder. Early on Monday morning, December 13, 1971, one witness testified, Nauss awakened him and led him to a garage behind his apartment house. The man followed him into a loft upstairs in the garage, where Nauss, holding a candle for illumination, directed his friend's attention upward. There was Liz Lande's nude and bludgeoned body hanging by her neck from a rope strung over a beam.

"See what I've done," the witness quoted Nauss to the court. "She won't bother me anymore."

"Her head was off to one side," the witness remembered on the stand. "And her tongue was hanging out. It was a terrible sight." He went on to relate how Nauss threatened that "something could happen to your wife" if the friend didn't then help him remove and bury Liz Lande. They wrapped her in a sheet and carried her downstairs to the friend's car. It was difficult to jam Liz's rigid body in the trunk.

They then drove the short distance to a forested area near Atco, New Jersey, where they stopped near the road and got out shovels to dig Liz Lande's grave. They finished and were about to return to the car to fetch the body when a motorist drove up and for some unknown reason began to inspect the car closely. When the stranger drove on, Nauss and his unwilling accomplice left, too, for an even more remote burial site.

Later, according to another witness, Nauss returned to the grave and dug up his dead girlfriend. To ensure that she could not be identified, he severed her hands and feet and used pliers to extract all her teeth. Elizabeth Lande's remains never have been recovered.

The following narrative was prepared by Alan LeFebvre, the public information officer for the Pennyslvania State Correctional Institution at Graterford:

> Robert Nauss was sentenced to life and twenty to forty years in prison for the ... death of his girlfriend Elizabeth Ann Lande. He was received at Graterford on August 22, 1979, to begin serving this sentence. His adjustment to incarceration was relatively uneventful in terms of behavior problems or related concerns. Shortly after his arrival he took a job in the prison's hobby shop, an area where inmates under the supervision of a civilian staff member make a variety of items for resale to the community, and various furniture items which are ordered by staff or members of the general public.
>
> While in the hobby shop Nauss became good friends with Hans VorHauer, a forty-one-year-old inmate serving thirteen and a half to twenty-seven years for robbery and a variety of other related offenses. Vor-

Hauer was considered to be an excellent cabinet maker. In August of 1983, the institution received an order for a chest to be built and delivered by Christmas to a family in Philadelphia. The hobby-shop supervisor gave VorHauer the task of designing and constructing this piece of furniture. The chest was of furniture-grade lumber and skillfully crafted and built. As it turns out, *it was also capable of concealing Robert Nauss and Hans VorHauer.* [Emphasis added.]

After several weeks of work the chest was ready for shipment. On the afternoon of November 17, 1983, inmates from the hobby shop either wittingly or unwittingly rolled the chest out, with Nauss and VorHauer concealed inside, through the main gate, where it was loaded onto a waiting U-Haul van, which drove off the prison grounds headed for Philadelphia.

VorHauer was captured on November 11, 1986, and is now back in prison serving his original sentence. . . . Nauss remains on the run despite the coordinated efforts of the Pennsylvania State Police and the U.S. Marshals Service.

No one in the Marshals Service is ready to concede that Robert Nauss may be gone for good. "We will get Nauss," investigator Thomas C. Rapone has told Harry Maitland of the Delaware County (Pennsylvania) *Daily Times.* Rapone and others believe that Nauss has received help over the years from various biker gangs and that he has probably supported himself, at least in part, by making and selling drugs as

Hans VorHauer did before his recapture. Furthermore, warns Rapone, Nauss is clever enough to blend into the sort of suburban background he knew as a youth.

To compensate for Nauss's chameleonlike ability to pass as either an aging yuppie or low-life biker, the marshals have commissioned a bust of their quarry, created to reflect how he might look today, aged eleven years since his last photo. The forensic artist who fashioned the bust, Frank Bender of Philadelphia, also did the likeness of recently convicted family killer John List from New Jersey. A witness, Wanda Flanery of Denver, saw the List likeness on TV and recognized it as "Bob Clark," her former neighbor in Denver's Montbello area. A call to the FBI led to List's May 1989 apprehension in Virginia, eighteen years after he slaughtered his mother, his wife and their three children.

It is to be hoped that the marshals enjoy similar success in their hunt for Robert Nauss.

4. Killing Cousins

WILFREDO RODRÍGUEZ
Irvington Township, New Jersey

DATE OF BIRTH: NOVEMBER 8, 1963
HEIGHT: FIVE FEET, EIGHT INCHES
WEIGHT: 125 POUNDS
HAIR: BLACK
EYES: BROWN
DISTINGUISHING MARKS OR SCARS: TATTOO ON UPPER RIGHT
   ARM
ALSO KNOWN AS: WILFREDO, ROBERTO ORTIZ, WILFREDO
   RODRÍGUEZ SANTANA
REWARD: NONE
CONTACT: IRVINGTON POLICE DEPARTMENT
           (201) 399-6541

In 1983, 528 Grove Street was a habitable, if unappealing, address in a third-rate neighborhood of a decaying slum, Irvington Township, hard by the shabbier districts of Newark, New Jersey. The area is even worse today.

Still, Alfredo Ortiz's three-story residence on Grove, across from a beer-and-shot joint called Mazur's, was in better shape than most houses in the vicinity, and more importantly, the hardworking Puerto Rican native owned the building. Ortiz rented the upstairs apartment to an elderly tenant, Ada Matías. Alfredo and his

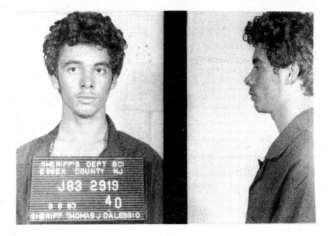

Wilfredo Rodríguez

frumpy wife María, thirty-nine, lived with their
three sons on the two floors below. In the basement, Alfredo's son by a previous marriage,
Luis, shared a bedroom with nineteen-year-old
Wilfredo Rodríguez, a cousin who had come
north from Lajas, the Ortiz's village in Puerto
Rico, to live with the family.

Alfredo Ortiz supported his family as a self-
employed carpenter and residential-building
contractor in the general Irvington area. He got
up early every morning and came home at the
same time every night. Ortiz, in short, was un-
exceptionable and steady, by all accounts a
loving husband and dependable breadwinner.

María, alas, was said to lack these virtues.
Although she was hardly a looker—a local
cop describes Mrs. Ortiz as "short, fat and

dumpy"—she seems to have stirred young Wilfredo Rodríguez, who allegedly was her lover. Afternoons while Alfredo wearily toiled in the renovation of Irvington's crumbling houses (and Wilfredo was supposedly working in a scissors factory), the pair reportedly trysted their time away. And while they dallied, say the police, the young man and older woman allegedly were plotting to kill Alfredo.

According to the official theory of the case, the lovers' decision to slay María's husband may have been hastened by Alfredo's discovery of their affair. The police know for certain that in late May of 1983 the Ortizes began to argue bitterly with one another, and that Wilfredo physically interceded in one of their fights. A week following this altercation, Alfredo gave his wife's boyfriend until June 10 to vacate 528 Grove. On the morning of June 7, the Ortizes started battling again. This time, Alfredo threatened to stab María. After he'd stormed off to work, says a police detective familiar with the case, María told an unnamed third party that Alfredo was overdue for a stabbing himself.

At about nine that night, within the clear and horrified sight of old Mrs. Matías upstairs, Wilfredo Rodríguez jumped Alfredo Ortiz in front of his house with a plastic-handled, twelve-inch folding blade known locally as an "007 knife." Mrs. Matías watched Ortiz run around the corner into an alley, where Wilfredo caught up with the older man and stabbed him seventeen times in his back, chest, arms, head and face. Alfredo stumbled on for about a block before falling dead in a pool of his own blood.

Ada Matías was afraid of María Ortiz, say the cops, and was so intimidated by the newly minted widow that she at first would say nothing about what she saw that night. Both María and Wilfredo were questioned by the police and released.

According to the same sources, Maria also endeavored to cow Luis, her stepson, into silence, threatening to murder the boy should he tell the authorities anything of what he knew about his father's death. Then she and Wilfredo flew off together for rest and recreation in Puerto Rico. No sooner had they departed, however, than Luis went to the cops with his story. As a result, the police were able to get arrest warrants on the vacationers, not for murder—yet—but for making death threats against Luis Ortiz.

The lovers' arrests on these charges upon their return to Irvington appear to have emboldened Ada Matías. She finally told authorities what she had seen, testimony that led to indictments on February 10, 1984. Wilfredo was charged with the murder itself, plus conspiracy to commit it, possession of a weapon for unlawful purposes and other felonies. Maria, the alleged temptress, was also accused of conspiracy as well as harboring a fugitive and hindering his apprehension.

Then justice was bushwhacked once again, this time in the courts. "Quite frankly," explains a New Jersey prosecutor knowledgeable about the ensuing developments, "this case has defied logic."

In April, Wilfredo and María were put on trial together. She was acquitted of all charges save that of harboring a fugitive. He was also acquitted of conspiracy, but was found guilty on all other counts. Pending the outcome of their appeals, both parties were granted bail. María made hers and then put up the family house as collateral on Wilfredo's. On July 30, 1984, he walked free.

The appeals process moves slowly just about everywhere, but for Wilfredo Rodríguez its pace in New Jersey was glacial. On March 27, 1987, Wilfredo's murder conviction was affirmed and he was ordered to surrender. At the time, he and María were living in nearby Kearny, New Jersey. He ignored the order for four months until both of them were picked up on bench warrants.

Two months later, an appellate court ordered Rodríguez released on bail once again, pending determination of his further appeals. That decision came down eight days later. Finally, and unequivocally, Wilfredo Rodríguez had run out of legal gas. Of course, he had also run out of town by this time, and has stayed gone, perhaps in Puerto Rico. María Ortiz, say police, is probably with him.

5. "A Real New York City Con Man"

WILLIAM PETER FISCHER
Southampton, New York

DATE OF BIRTH: OCTOBER 4, 1944
HEIGHT: FIVE FEET, ELEVEN INCHES
WEIGHT: 185 POUNDS
HAIR: SALT-AND-PEPPER
EYES: BLUE
DISTINGUISHING MARKS OR SCARS: TRACHEOTOMY SCAR, "MARY" TATTOED ON RIGHT BICEPS
OTHER: FAVORS HEAVY GOLD JEWELRY; SUFFERS FROM AN ACID STOMACH; CHAIN-SMOKES MENTHOL FILTER CIGARETTES; APT TO BE WORKING AS A CAR SALESMAN
REWARD: THE NEW YORK STATE POLICE WILL PAY AN UNSPECIFIED AMOUNT FOR INFORMATION LEADING TO FISCHER'S ARREST.
CONTACT: NEW YORK STATE POLICE
(800) 262-4321

Bill Fischer was a man of stark and troubling contrasts.

In retrospect, it is clear that no one really knew who he was or what he might do. Certainly no one believed him capable of murdering his own son.

A neighbor in the exclusive Long Island beach

William Peter Fischer

community of Southampton remembered Fischer in *Newsday* as "a perfect neighbor and a nice guy." Bill's former boss at a Manhattan car dealership concurred. "He was a likable person," the dealer recalled, "a generous person, always a handshake and a smile." Yet Fischer's immediate family, including two ex-wives, had different tales to tell, especially about those times when Bill was drinking or taking cocaine. "Moody, irritable and unpredictable" is how one cop described the family consensus on Fischer to the newspaper.

Brooklyn-born Bill Fischer was never a stranger to trouble. His father, James, sold cars and was a drunk, and so was Bill's mother. Bill's education stopped in high school, and he did prison time for car theft as a youth. Yet with that ready handshake and winning smile (just like his dad) and that confident four-square look of sincerity, Fischer was able to rise above his beginnings. He could sell himself, and he could sell things, particularly automobiles (just like his dad). In good years, according to one published account, Fischer earned $100,000 or more.

But neither the money nor his friendly manner compensated for a fundamental flaw in Fischer's character. "As we delved into his background," says Lieutenant Gene Corcoran of the New York State Police, "we found that he had no long-term relations with people, or any real friendships. He was mostly flash, street smart, a real New York City con man."

By the mid-1980s Fischer's first marriage was long since ended and his second one was falling apart. He was the father of two sons by his first wife, but it had been years since he'd communicated directly with her or with the boys. The estrangement probably was just as well because there had been violence in the household when Bill was at home and particularly ill will between him and Bill Jr., who was born in 1967. When the youngster developed terminal cystic fibrosis, his father balked at helping with the considerable medical expenses.

Bill Jr. therefore was taking something of a risk in contacting his dad in December of 1986. Friends speculate that he might have been in desperate need of money. Whatever reason he gave his father for wanting to see him, Bill Sr. agreed to a meeting and even invited his son to dinner with Dad at Fischer's nine-room house in Southampton. The date was set for December 11—a Thursday—and apparently everything went smoothly at first. As Raymond Neuman, a next-door neighbor, recalled to reporter Shirley Perlman of *Newsday*, the elder Fischer invited Neuman to go fishing with him and his boy in the morning, but Neuman declined because of the bad weather that day. At midafternoon, Neuman continued, he saw the two Bills coming home. They were singing "Jingle Bells" together.

Young Bill, who didn't drive, had arranged for twenty-one-year-old Nancy Hyer, a computer technician he'd recently met, to pick him up after dinner. Nancy drove her mother's car to Fischer's house. It was a 1981 two-door, white Pontiac.

The only available account of the evening, Bill Fischer, Sr.'s, would prove spare. He told investigators that Bill Jr. ate with him and that

Nancy Hyer and his son departed together at about 9:30 P.M. No person reported seeing the two alive after that hour. Ten days later, police discovered the Hyer Pontiac, parked and locked behind the Elks Club in Southampton, within walking distance of Fischer's house.

Bill Jr. and Nancy were found—murdered— in the automobile's trunk.

The boy was clad in a gray pullover, black pants and moccasins, and had been shot eighteen times in his head and chest with a .22-caliber weapon. An autopsy determined that he had been dragged over rocks, somewhere, before being placed in the car trunk. Nancy Hyer was stuffed in the trunk next to him. She was nude and wrapped in a blanket. Ms. Hyer had been stabbed in the heart and liver.

Neither murder weapon was ever recovered.

William Fischer's horror and bereavement at the double murder initially appeared genuine. His first wife—the slain boy's mother—came to stay with her ex-husband for Christmas and for their son's funeral. In early January, she drove Fischer to the hospital because she feared his despondency was deepening into a suicidal urge. During the same period a neighbor, also worried about Fischer's mental state, took his pistol away. The weapon didn't work.

"I remember one day at his house he started crying," says Lieutenant Corcoran of the state police. "He handed me a Mass card with his son's picture on it and said, 'I want you to keep this to help motivate the guys to catch the person who killed my son.' Later, I learned from people who knew him that Fischer has the trick of making himself cry whenever he wants."

Disclosures of this sort, plus the absolute lack of any other suspect in the case, soon focused police attention on the supposedly grieving William Fischer, Sr. A warrant to search his house was obtained. On December 31, ten days after the bodies were found, detectives confiscated, among other items, the contents of Fischer's vacuum cleaner. Tests revealed dried blood inside the appliance, along with the usual dust and debris. The blood matched that of Nancy Hyer. Paint chips were also recovered from the house. They were similar to paint chips found on the blanket in which the girl's body was wrapped.

With these results in hand, two more searches were conducted on January 16 and 17, 1987. More dried blood of unknown origin was found, plus two spent slugs. Stuck to one bullet was a hair microscopically indistinguishable from Bill Jr.'s Also, an examination of Fischer's bedroom walls disclosed traces of three freshly repaired bullet holes.

Such strong physical evidence is usually sufficient to justify an arrest warrant. But this was a highly unusual homicide case; the authorities did not want to act precipitously. Although both young Bill Fischer and Nancy Hyer almost certainly were brutally murdered inside his father's house, the fact that she was stabbed and he was shot was baffling to detectives. A single killer in such a setting rarely employs two different weapons. The police wondered if Bill Sr. was protecting someone, an accomplice perhaps. Another possibility, considered far-fetched, is that young Bill killed Nancy and was then slain by his father.

What, in fact, did happen that night? "This has been gone over by a lot of good detectives," says Lieutenant Corcoran. "And it's almost impossible to say. Who killed whom first? Did he kill both of them? I don't think anyone but Bill Fischer can answer that."

Corcoran nevertheless has his own theories. "My opinion," he says, "would be that it was a crime of rage, based on the crime scene and based on his relationship with his son and based on our information that he was prone to fits of rage and losing his temper. In my opinion he had a falling-out with his son and he flew into a violent rage. And there is absolutely no doubt in my mind that the girl was a totally innocent victim."

Bill Fischer, Sr., of course, might shed a great deal of light on this mystery—if the police could find him. After the three searches of his house, the cops went to Fischer's local attorney to ask, bluntly, if his client, their suspect, required a tail. Were they going to have to follow Fischer around, or would he surrender for questioning—or indictment—should such come to pass? They were assured that Fischer would make himself available upon request.

In the meantime, according to what he told the law and his lawyer, Fischer needed money to pay for his defense. That is why no one became seriously suspicious in early February 1987, when he took out a $160,000 second mortgage on his Southampton house.

It is unfortunate that suspicions were not aroused, however, because Bill Fischer was on his way out of town. On February 10, he paid a social call on his stepmother in Farmingdale,

Long Island, and that was the last anyone saw of him. The next afternoon his blue Mercedes was recovered from a parking lot at Kennedy International Airport. Two weeks later, a Long Island grand jury indicted William Peter Fischer on two counts of second-degree murder.

6. Not a Murderer But . . .

EDWARD EDGAR NYE
Columbia County, New York

DATE OF BIRTH: JUNE 30, 1945
HEIGHT: FIVE FEET, ELEVEN INCHES
WEIGHT: 210 POUNDS
HAIR: BROWN
EYES: BROWN
DISTINGUISHING MARKS OR SCARS: APPENDECTOMY SCAR
ALIAS: NONE KNOWN
LAST SEEN: ALBANY, NEW YORK, FEBRUARY 1983
REWARD: THE NEW YORK STATE POLICE WILL PAY AN UN-
    SPECIFIED AMOUNT FOR INFORMATION LEADING TO NYE'S
    ARREST.
CONTACT: NEW YORK STATE POLICE
          (800) 262-4321

Capital homicide is the ultimate felony; there is no more reprehensible crime than premeditated, cold-blooded murder. Yet many police detectives say they'd prefer any day to investigate a homicide, no matter how grisly, rather than a rape, for example, or an instance of incest or a pedophilia case. Reason: Murder, for all its horror, is a crime of finality. No matter how depraved or brutal a murder is, the victim

159

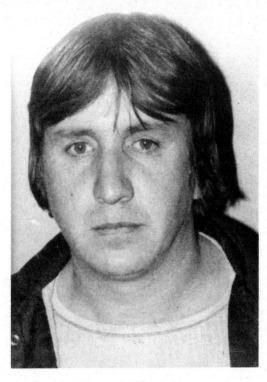

Edward Edgar Nye

is *gone,* reducible in a detective's mind to an abstraction, a stack of reports, photos and some items in an evidence locker.

This necessary professional detachment is much more difficult to achieve with living victims, especially those who have suffered sexual violence. These people survive to endure their continuing trauma daily, and they often force investigating officers to share the burden of their awesome, sometimes permanent, psychic damage. Such cases can take a heavy emotional toll on cops.

When the "perp" (for perpetrator) is an adult male and his victim a boy, there is the added tragedy that this type of sexual violence frequently begets itself. Many, if not most, victims of man-boy sex crimes will themselves, in time, become offenders themselves. Crime experts also point out three other common characteristics of "chicken hawks," as they are sometimes called. One, their desire for victims tends to intensify rather than moderate as they age. One infamous offender, a man in his fifties, once boasted to his captors of his sexual intimacy with more than 5,000 victims. Two, as these men grow older they tend to pursue younger and younger victims. And three, it is not unusual for the deviant urge to become so demanding—or the perceived need to cover up these crimes so pressing—that the encounters naturally escalate into the ultimate felony, murder.

These are among the reasons why the New York State Police requested that Edward E. Nye be included with the convicted, accused and suspected murderers in this book.

Nye was born near Albany, New York. According to what one of his brothers later told state police investigators, their father sexually abused young Eddy, who was placed in the first of a series of foster homes at an early age.

As an adult, Nye settled first in the village of Middleburg, New York, southeast of Albany.

There he worked at odd jobs, including carpet installation. He did some car-repair work, too. His primary interests, however, were the rock band he formed (Eddy sang, patterning himself after Elvis) and weight lifting. Nye was very muscular, an avid physical culturist who encouraged the younger boys in Middleburg to work out with his set of weights too. He even helped them design their individual weight-training programs.

If Nye was an active pedophile at this time (his twenties and early thirties), it is not reflected in the local police files, where there is a single entry, a burglary charge that was later dropped. Yet his interest in young men and boys apparently did not go unnoticed. Some years later, says Pat Donnelly, the state police investigator in charge of the Nye case, a woman who knew Nye in Middleburg would remember in a letter to the local newspaper that Eddy "was around the village chasing little boys, attracting them with flashy cars and flashy dress and manner. He always tried to look younger than he was."

In time Nye departed Middleburg, possibly because of local suspicions, and next appeared in rural Columbia County, which lies south of Albany along the Hudson River. He had been hired as a counselor at a minimum-security correctional farm for boys.

Not long thereafter—early in 1981—several of the boys, all aged fifteen or sixteen, came forward with allegations of homosexual advances by Mr. Nye. On January 13, 1982, he was arrested in the matter and formally charged with thirty-two counts of sodomy, which is defined in the New York penal code as "deviant sexual intercourse."

A year passed before Nye's case was ready for adjudication. On February 4, 1983, under an arrangement worked out with the court, he pleaded guilty to two counts of sexual abuse and two counts of the more serious charge of sodomy. Eddy Nye was to serve from two to six years in prison, and his formal sentencing was scheduled for later in the month. In the interim, he was admitted to the lock-down wards at Albany's Capital District Psychiatric Center.

While an in-patient at the center, Nye was identified as potentially suicidal, a not uncommon condition among new prisoners frightened for their physical safety in prison. As it turned out, however, Eddy didn't have any worries.

Either by chance or design, his "in-patient" designation at the center was altered to read "out-patient" just a few days before he was due for sentencing. Suddenly free to leave whenever he liked, Nye went home to his apartment in Albany (which he shared with a female companion). There, he gathered up his gear and held a garage sale, which netted him about $1,000. On February 23, when officers arrived at the psychiatric center to take Eddy Nye to court, he was long gone.

Nye, who may have relocated to New York City, did not vanish entirely. And apparently he did not relish his life as a fugitive. In the months following his escape he telephoned a Columbia County private detective, inquiring if there was any way his sentence could be set aside. Nye also contacted his court-appointed lawyer with the same questions. No negotiations or deal proposals were ever made.

Now, more than seven years later, Eddy's trail is cold.

"Do I think he's still alive?" asks Pat Donnelly rhetorically. "Certainly I do." Furthermore, says the state police investigator who took over the case in 1987, if Eddy still wants to talk about his case, Donnelly is willing to listen to what he might have in mind.

"As far as I'm concerned, it's negotiable," says Donnelly.

7. The Revolutionary

JOANNE CHESIMARD
New Brunswick, New Jersey

DATE OF BIRTH: JULY 16, 1947
HEIGHT: FIVE FEET, EIGHT INCHES
WEIGHT: 126 TO 138 POUNDS
HAIR: BLACK
EYES: BROWN
DISTINGUISHING MARKS OR SCARS: ROUND SCAR ON LEFT KNEE AND VARIOUS BULLET WOUNDS UNDER RIGHT ARM AND LEFT SHOULDER
ALSO KNOWN AS: JOANNE BYRON, JOANNE CHESTERMAN, MARY DAVIS, JOSEPHINE HENDERSON, JUSTINE HENDERSON, BARBARA ODOMA, ASSATA SHAKUR
REWARD: NONE
CONTACT: NEW JERSEY STATE POLICE
FUGITIVE UNIT
(609) 882-2000 EXT. 2780

Back in the late 1960s and early 1970s, the Black Liberation Army was a fierce and tight-knit underground organization of self-styled urban guerrillas who portrayed themselves as radical warriors in the fight against white exploitation and oppression in the United States. Law enforcement agencies demurred. Noting that the group's principal activities included bank robberies and armored-car heists, the cops

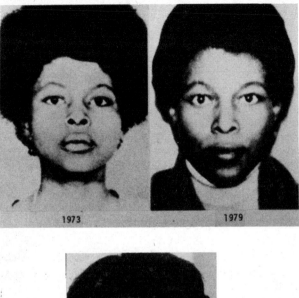

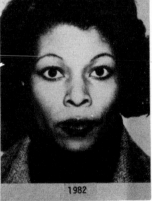

1982

Joanne Chesimard   (credit: AP/Wideworld)

regarded the Black Liberation Army as a fancy term for a bunch of violence-prone thieves.

The BLA's animating force—their "soul" as the *New York Times* put it—was Joanne Chesimard. Her active life as a revolutionary blossomed in 1971 when she was alleged to have taken part in the April 5 stickup at the Hilton Hotel in New York City. She was later implicated in BLA bank jobs in the Bronx and Queens, New York.

Then the charges grew more serious. Early in 1973, she was accused of attempting to murder a Queens policeman (this charge was later dropped) and also of participating in the abduction and killing of a New York drug dealer. Chesimard was acquitted on the kidnap beef and was never brought to trial for the dealer's slaying.

That spring, Chesimard achieved her enduring infamy (or fame, as some fellow radicals understood it) by participating in the murder of a New Jersey state trooper. After dark on May 2, she was driving south on the New Jersey turnpike in a white Pontiac with her lover, James Coston, also known as Zayd Shakur. He had previously acted as information minister for the Black Panthers. Also in the Pontiac was another male, Clark Squires, who answered to the name of Sundiata Acoli.

New Jersey state trooper James M. Harper, twenty-nine, later testified that he pulled Chesimard over after noticing that the Pontiac's headlights weren't working properly. When he asked her for identification, said the trooper, Chesimard pulled a handgun. Chesimard denied this.

Whoever's correct, there is no doubt that a gun battle occurred in which Harper was wounded and another trooper, thirty-four-year-old Werner Foerster, was killed. Coston, a.k.a. Shakur, also died in the shoot-out. Chesimard, whom police records indicate was armed that evening with a Browning nine-millimeter automatic, a .38-caliber Llama and a .38-caliber Browning automatic, sustained wounds in her chest, collarbone and arm.

Two months later, while awaiting trial, she smuggled a tape recording, entitled "To My People," from her cell. In it, Chesimard apologized for the incident as an example of her poor revolutionary discipline. "I should have known better," she said on the tape, which was aired on radio stations and played at militants' gatherings. "The turnpike is a checkpoint where black people are stopped, searched, harassed and assaulted. Revolutionaries must never be in too much of a hurry or make careless decisions. He who runs when the sun is sleeping will stumble many times." Chesimard reaffirmed her radicalism, proclaiming "war on the rich who prosper on our poverty, the politicians who lie to us with smiling faces and all the mindless, heartless robots who protect them and their property."

About six months later, in an anteroom of the federal courthouse in Queens where she faced trial on one of her old bank robbery charges, Joanne Chesimard and a mystery companion conceived a child. The little girl, named Kakuya, weighed six pounds at birth on September 11, 1974, in the prison ward of the Elmhurst Hospital Center in Queens. Her mother subsequently was convicted of trooper Foerster's murder in a New Brunswick, New Jersey, court and was sentenced to a life term plus sixty-five years.

Chesimard, as is usual for long-term inmates, was moved from prison to prison over the coming years before being transferred, in April of 1979, from a federal facility in West Virginia to the Clinton Correctional Institution for Women, a minimum-security facility in the hills of western New Jersey, about fifteen miles east of the Pennsylvania border. At Clinton, she was held with six other women in a cellblock known as South Hall, a one-story yellow-brick structure enclosed by a chain-link fence topped with two feet of barbed wire.

On Friday, November 2 of that year, a male caller arrived at Clinton and checked into the registration building. He was not searched, but escorted by prison van to South Hall and admitted inside, where he met with Ms. Chesimard in a glass-enclosed booth. Then two more male visitors arrived. They were not searched, either. Instead, the same guard who escorted the first man to South Hall drove the new pair of callers to the cellblock's front door. There, one of the two produced a gun and took the guard prisoner. Inside, the man visiting Chesimard drew two handguns and directed the female guard standing outside the glass booth to open the door.

Then all six people—Chesimard, her three males callers and the two guards—rode the prison van across a wide field to an adjoining school for the mentally handicapped. There, in the parking lot, were two waiting vehicles. The guards were freed, unharmed. Chesimard and her liberators fled in the getaway cars to Interstate 78, about 200 yards from the prison gates, which they took in to Pennsylvania.

As she later explained in her 1987 book, *Assata*, Chesimard then secretly worked her way south along the Atlantic coast with the aid of the Black Panther underground. Her first destination was Florida, then Central America and, finally, Fidel Castro's workers' paradise, Cuba, where Joanne Chesimard is believed to be today.

8. "You Better Pray for Me"

DONALD EUGENE PERKINS
Saxonburg, Pennsylvania

DATE OF BIRTH: JULY 14, 1931
HEIGHT: FIVE FEET, NINE INCHES
WEIGHT: 165 POUNDS
HAIR: GRAY-BROWN
EYES: BROWN
DISTINGUISHING MARKS OR SCARS: SMALL SCARS ON RIGHT CHEEK AND RIGHT FOREARM; "DON" ALLEGEDLY TATTOOED ON WEB OF RIGHT HAND, "ANN" ON HIS CHEST
ALSO KNOWN AS: A. D. BAKER, DONALD EUGENE PIERCE, STANLEY J. PIERCE, JOHN S. PORTAS, STANLEY JOHN PORTAS, BEV WEBB, EUGENE BEVLIN WEBB, EUGENE DONALD WEBB, STANLEY WEBB AND OTHERS
OTHER: PERKINS IS REPUTEDLY A MASTER OF DISGUISE; HE IS ALLERGIC TO PENICILLIN.
REWARD: NONE
CONTACT: NEAREST FBI OFFICE

Donald Perkins (the FBI knows him by his alias Donald Eugene Webb) is an Oklahoma City native. His legitimate occupations have included work as a butcher, restaurant manager, vending-machine repairman and auto, jewelry

 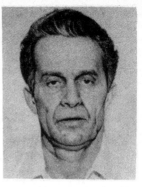

Donald Eugene Perkins

and real-estate salesman. But Perkins's avocation is felony. A former member of a gang of thieves and burglars that operated out of the Falls River, Massachusetts, area in the 1970s, he has been convicted of burglary, possession of counterfeit money, possession of a weapon, breaking and entering, armed robbery and car theft. In 1981, the FBI placed him on the Bureau's "Ten Most Wanted" list for the brutal 1980 murder of the Saxonburg, Pennsylvania, police chief.

At that time, according to authorities, Perkins made a regular yearly circuit of the eastern seaboard, casing, robbing or burglarizing jewelry stores from Kennebunkport to Key West. It was this business, they surmise, that brought him to Saxonburg, just north of Pittsburgh, on the afternoon of December 4, 1980.

He stopped in to a local jewelry exchange and examined a few pieces, tarrying long enough for the clerk to later make a positive identification of him. It appears, however, that for some reason he decided not to hazard a stickup. Law enforcement officials believe Perkins was heading out of town when he climbed back into his white sedan with Massachusetts plates and then gunned the vehicle down a Saxonburg street.

He ran a stop sign in the direct view of police chief Gregory B. Adams, who was coming in the opposite direction in his cruiser. According to Gordon Mainhart, the present chief of police in Saxonburg, Adams pulled a quick U-turn and took off after the out-of-state car.

Witnesses to the chase reported that Perkins maintained about a one-block lead over the pursuing Chief Adams until he suddenly veered into a feed-store parking lot, trying to hide. At first the ruse worked. Chief Adams went blazing by, but just caught a glimpse of the Massachusetts vehicle in the parking lot behind him. The policeman pulled another U-turn and returned to the lot, where he tried to block Perkins's vehicle.

"We don't know what happened next, except by conjecture," says Gordon Mainhart. "The next thing we knew a neighbor called 911 and told us an officer has been badly wounded."

The caller was Mrs. Midge Freehling, who did not see the incident, but who heard Chief Adams calling for help. Mrs. Freehling told her son, Tiger, to dial 911 while she went to the fallen policeman. Adams had two .25-caliber slugs in him and had been severely beaten around his face and head with a blunt instrument. "When I got to him, I could see he was in pretty bad shape," she later told a television interviewer. "But I told him, 'You'll be okay, honey.'

"He said, 'I don't think so. You better pray for me.'"

Two hours later, Chief Gregory Adams died of his injuries in a local hospital.

There has not been a single confirmed sighting of Donald Perkins since.

9. Bar Fight

HARRY SEGERQUIST
Watertown, Massachusetts

DATE OF BIRTH: NOVEMBER 23, 1929
HEIGHT: FIVE FEET, NINE INCHES
WEIGHT: 160 POUNDS
HAIR: BROWN
EYES: HAZEL
DISTINGUISHING MARKS OR SCARS: SHRAPNEL WOUND ON
   BACK, VACCINATION SCAR ON UPPER LEFT ARM
ALSO KNOWN AS: HARRY BURKE, HARRY LINDBURG, NILS
   NORDSTROM, JR., HARRY NILS SWANSON
OTHER: WEARS GLASSES, POSSIBLE HEART CONDITION
REWARD: NONE
CONTACT: MASSACHUSETTS DEPARTMENT OF CORRECTION
         FUGITIVE APPREHENSION UNIT
         (617) 727-2181

Since it was established in 1983, the Fugitive
Apprehension Unit within the Massachusetts
Department of Correction has caught more than
1,800 fugitives. Of the 255 prison escapees and
other felons wanted by various Massachusetts
police jurisdictions in '83, all but 14 have been
returned to custody. Among those still at large,
says Captain Curtis Wood, commander of the
Fugitive Apprehension Unit, he is particularly

Harry Segerquist

eager to retake the fugitive cop killer Harry Segerquist.

Harry's mother, the Swedish-born former Frideborg Lindberg, married John Segerquist of Stockholm in 1921. She bore two daughters before emigrating with her husband to New York City in 1928. According to information developed by Captain Wood's team, Frideborg had a roving eye, a predilection that led to extramarital adventures which, in late 1929, led to the birth of her son Harry, who in time would take his biological father's name and be known as Harry Nils Swanson.

John and Frideborg Segerquist separated in 1936 and were divorced three years later. As far as the Massachusetts authorities can determine, John Segerquist disappeared at about that time, and his ex-wife went to work in the New York area as a domestic servant. Harry would later tell prison officials that he last saw his sisters in 1937, and that he broke off direct contact with his mother in 1945.

He still called himself Harry Swanson when he joined the U.S. Marines in 1950. He was sent to Korea, where he was wounded in the back by shrapnel. He was awarded a Purple Heart. Harry also completed his high school education in the marines before being given, as his service record indicates, an "other than honorable" discharge on May 28, 1957, "pursuant to the sentence of the special court-martial for unauthorized absence."

In the meantime he had married a Jean Gilmore. Two children were born of the union. Two years after he was thrown out of the marines, Jean had Harry arrested for nonsupport of her and the children, and also for shacking up with another, unnamed female. He was picked up on a similar charge in 1962.

Then, says Captain Wood, Harry's record stayed clean for several years. He and his first wife divorced. In 1964, he began living with Ann Margaret Burke of Somerville, Massachusetts. Harry introduced Ms. Burke as his wife, but no marriage certificate has ever been found. He found work at various times as an air-conditioning and refrigeration repairman and as a mechanic and salesman.

For reasons known only to Mr. Segerquist-Swanson, in the late 1960s he began calling himself Nils Nordstrom, Jr. This was the name he gave on Monday night, July 21, 1969, when he stopped at Greg's Café on Mt. Auburn Street in Watertown, Massachusetts, for a drink. The apartment he shared with Ann Burke at 19 Cushing Street in Cambridge wasn't more than 150 yards from Greg's front door. When Harry-Nils walked into Greg's at about 7:30, he met four men at the bar. Two were off-duty Cambridge city cops, John Daly and Austin Jordan, who had been drinking there since 5:30.

For most Americans, *the* prime topic that night was astronaut Neil Armstrong's moon walk, then being beamed back to earth. But at the bar at Greg's, Officer Austin Jordan and "Nils Nordstrom" started arguing back and forth over another event of three days before—the drowning death of Mary Jo Kopechne in an auto driven off a bridge at Chappaquiddick on Martha's Vineyard, Massachusetts, by Senator Edward M. Kennedy, who failed to report the accident for ten hours.

Austin Jordan took a very dim view of Ted Kennedy's behavior that night. Nils Nordstrom staunchly defended the senator. Their debate heated up until Nordstrom became so enraged with Jordan that he announced he was going home to get his handgun. At 9:20 he was back at Greg's and exchanged further unpleasantries with the cop. Finally, he and Jordan walked outside together.

Minutes later, the patrons at Greg's heard a double pistol report from just outside the bar. Austin Jordan, clutching his stomach, crashed back through the front door and collapsed on the barroom floor. He was taken by ambulance to Mt. Auburn Hospital and died there a short time later.

There were several witnesses to the shooting

and its immediate aftermath, enough to narrow the police investigation that night to Nils Nordstrom. The .44 that killed Austin Jordan was discovered in Nordstrom's possession. He was arrested for the murder and tried and convicted on March 12, 1970.

Four years later, on March 27, 1974, Nils Nordstrom was granted a twelve-hour furlough from the correctional institution at Norfolk to visit his supposed wife, Ann Margaret Burke. Neither he nor she has been seen since. Captain Curtis Wood and his team continue to search for the pair. Wood believes they have remained together, and the hunt for them is centered in Florida.

SECTION FOUR

SOUTH AND SOUTHEAST

1. An Afternoon Lark

HARRY DANA BRASWELL, JR.
Live Oak, Florida

DATE OF BIRTH: JANUARY 7, 1958
HEIGHT: SIX FEET
WEIGHT: 150 POUNDS
HAIR: BROWN
EYES: GREEN
DISTINGUISHING MARKS OR SCARS: INITIALS ''HDB'' AND A
   HEART TATTOOED ON LEFT ARM
ALSO KNOWN AS: ''MOODY''
REWARD: NONE
CONTACT: FLORIDA DEPARTMENT OF LAW ENFORCEMENT
         MOST WANTED FUGITIVE HOTLINE
         (904) 487-0932
         OR
         (800) 342-7768 (INSIDE FLORIDA)
         OR
         SUWANNEE COUNTY SHERIFF ROBERT LEONARD
         (904) 362-2222

Sometimes, murder can erupt in the most casual and seemingly innocent of circumstances.

On a balmy spring day in 1975 in Live Oak, Florida, a quiet panhandle hamlet about ninety miles east of Tallahassee, high-schooler Harry Braswell, seventeen, decided to cut classes. Harry took his dad's car and was out cruising

Harry Dana Braswell in 1975, and three sketches drawn to suggest how he might have aged since.

around town when he saw three acquaintances, also truants, who waved at him from a teen hangout where they were drinking sodas. Harry, a new kid in town, pulled into the parking lot and conferred with the other boys for a bit. After a time, it was decided that they'd all get into the car and head with Harry for a nearby stretch of the Suwannee River.

In view of the crime that Harry and his friends were about to commit, it is logical to suspect that the boys were drinking something stronger than colas that afternoon, or perhaps were abusing other substances. According to Suwannee County sheriff Robert Leonard, however, the four youths consumed no alcohol or drugs.

But they did get the car stuck in the riverbank mud.

As they considered how to solve this problem, one of the boys recalled an acquaintance, an older man who lived in the area, frail and genial, seventy-year-old John Robinson, whose wife was gravely ill in the hospital. The foursome walked the short way to Robinson's house and prevailed upon the old fellow to let them borrow his car. What occurred next is not entirely clear, but it is known that instead of pulling the Braswell vehicle out of the mud, the boys pushed the car the rest of the way into the river, leaving deep tread marks that were easy to see.

Then they conceived a scheme wherein all four would take off west on Interstate 10—after they robbed John Robinson. Harry Braswell, the others later testified, led them back into the house, where they bound Robinson to a chair and tortured him with cigarette butts, hoping he'd disclose the location of his valuables. When it became clear that he had nothing, a pillowcase was placed over his head and John Robinson suffocated to death.

The youths (none of whom had any prior arrest record) did not ransack the house. They took an unspecified amount of cash, a small-caliber handgun and some whiskey—maybe—and then departed. That evening, about 120 miles northwest in Quincy, Florida, they were arrested and brought back to Live Oak for arraignment and trial. Weeks later, Harry Dana Braswell's three accomplices received relatively light prison terms for their part in the crime. Harry wasn't so fortunate. He was sentenced to life in prison, with a minimum of twenty-five years to be served before he could be considered for parole.

Braswell did not at first adjust well to confinement. His early record at Florida's Sumter Correctional Institution in Bushnell, a high-security facility for youthful offenders, is littered with so-called DPRs—Disciplinary Reports—for various rules infractions. Yet soon thereafter, Harry developed into a model inmate.

It was found that although his reading level was low, about ninth-grade, Harry was pretty bright; his IQ score at Sumter was 120. Within three years he had earned a high-school-equivalency diploma and was developing considerable expertise as an auto mechanic in the prison's vocational program. He also earned almost two years' worth of college credit in a self-study program offered by nearby Lake Sumter Junior College.

Each year his behavior marks were consistently high; had it not been for the heinousness of John Robinson's murder, Braswell might have been considered for an early work-release program. Still, he bore down. Harry became a crackerjack car repairman, then added skills in business office management and printing, including bindery operation and graphics.

Looking back, Braswell seemed to have been perhaps *too* motivated for a someone looking at a quarter century behind bars. And Harry, it turned out, *did* have other plans, escape schemes he was developing with another inmate, James Eric Knight. . . . Their escape is described in the next chapter.

2. A Corpse in the Canal

JAMES ERIC KNIGHT
Miami, Florida

DATE OF BIRTH: MARCH 5, 1959
HEIGHT: FIVE FEET, TEN INCHES
WEIGHT: 165 POUNDS
HAIR: BROWN
EYES: BROWN
REWARD: NONE
CONTACT: FLORIDA DEPARTMENT OF CORRECTIONS
WILLIAM SCHNITZER
(904) 488-0003

James Knight, eighteen, known by his middle name, Eric, lived with his mother, Lucille, in an upper-middle-class Miami, Florida, neighborhood. Mrs. Knight worked as a barmaid in a local pub. Eric made a few bucks mowing lawns and doing maintenance jobs. But what he was after was a big score, and it didn't seem to matter what he had to do to get it. That is why Miami postal worker and Boy Scout leader John Henry Sime, thirty-seven, is now dead.

John Sime, a natty dresser with expensive tastes in jewelry and cars, harbored one dark secret, his sexual preference for young boys. In the autumn of 1977, he called the Knight house, looking for Lucille's ex-husband, whom Sime had known in the

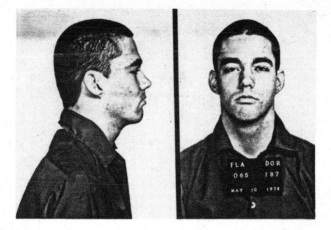

James Eric Knight

naval reserve. Instead, Eric answered the phone. According to the story Lucille Knight later told, Sime told Eric that he liked the boy's voice and said he thought they should get together. They did so the next day, in the Knight garage. As Eric would relate later it was a hurried assignation, consummated amid old TV sets, cars, broken furniture, a canoe and sundry refuse. Eric expected to be compensated for his services, but Sime put him off, promising instead to pay the teenager double for a second garage rendezvous they arranged for Sunday, November 20, 1977.

Early on the appointed day, Knight met with two friends, James Spencer, seventeen, and sixteen-year-old Ricky Fernández. Together, as Knight would tell the police, the three pals decided to rob Sime, reasoning that the older man wouldn't dare report the crime. Exactly what transpired in the Knight garage on the evening of the twentieth isn't known. But the consequences of the plot are. In the version offered by Knight's lawyer, Sime again refused to pay. Eric and Ricky Fernández (who had been hiding in the garage) then lost their heads and proceeded to bludgeon and choke Sime to death.

Miami Metro police detective Charles Majors recounted events somewhat differently. "There was no price involved," Majors told *Miami Herald* reporter Arnold Markowitz. "What the whole meeting was, as far as Knight was concerned, was a conspiracy to commit murder and robbery. The way Sime dressed and carried himself, and the fact that he drove a brand-new car, gave him the outside appearance of being well off."

Knight and his friends loaded Sime's battered body into a ratty pickup and sped with it to a secluded spot on West Canal, one of several such shallow waterways that crisscross the outskirts of Miami. At the canal they found a heavy, rusted-out air conditioner to which they strapped Sime before dumping him in the water. Because the canal wasn't deep enough to wholly conceal Sime, the boys then dumped some old tires on top of his cadaver, as well as a crate of rotting chicken parts.

Within a matter of days John Henry Sime floated up to the surface of West Canal, where he was discovered by a man dumping trash. Eric Knight subsequently gave himself up and confessed his role in the murder to homicide sergeant Dave Simmons. Although his attorneys would later argue that the confession was illegally obtained under duress, a jury nevertheless found Knight guilty of John Henry Sime's murder, as well as robbery. He was sentenced to a life term, and a consecutive ninety-nine years.

Because of his age, James Eric Knight was sent to the Sumter Correctional Institution, where he met Harry Dana Braswell, who'd been there for three years. Three years after that, in 1981, James and Harry began digging an escape tunnel from the rear of the print shop, where they both worked. Carefully secreting the dirt they removed into the print-shop walls and ceiling, Knight and Braswell managed to burrow nineteen feet before abandoning their project in early 1983.

A better idea, they decided, was to take the same route to freedom that Robert Nauss and Hans VorHauer chose. In this case, Knight and Braswell selected a heavy cabinet in the print shop and then requested that a flatbed truck come to haul the bulky cabinet away as junk. They monitored the cabinet's progress out through the prison gates, noting with glee that no one bothered to look inside it.

Some weeks later, on the afternoon of February 22, 1983, a second cabinet was hauled from the prison print shop to a garbage dump beyond the walls. This time, James and Harry were hidden inside it. When the abandoned cabinet was later searched, prison officials found a checklist of food and gear that the escapees took with them. It included matches, a flashlight, knives, clothing, ammonia and black pepper (to confuse any possible tracking dogs), backpacks, granola bars and honey.

The hand-scribbled list is the only trace of Braswell and Knight so far to turn up. "So much for our crack penal system," says Sergeant Simmons in Miami, a note of resignation in his voice.

3. The Lebanese Mafia

LEO JOSEPH KOURY
Richmond, Virginia

DATE OF BIRTH: JULY 14, 1934
HEIGHT: FIVE FEET, ELEVEN INCHES
WEIGHT: 240 POUNDS
HAIR: BLACK
EYES: BROWN
DISTINGUISHING MARKS OR SCARS: PINK BIRTHMARK BE-
NEATH RIGHT EYE
ALSO KNOWN AS: MIKE DECKER
OTHER: LEO KOURY IS A DIABETIC AND SUFFERS FROM A
HEART AILMENT. BOTH CONDITIONS REQUIRE PRESCRIP-
TION MEDICATION.
REWARD: $25,000
CONTACT: AGENT HENRY HANDY
RICHMOND, VIRGINIA, FBI OFFICE
(804) 261-1044

Law enforcement officials in Richmond, Virginia, have vivid recollections of the mid-1970s when their city, the old capital of the Confederacy, was under siege from within by a confederacy of thugs known to the cops as Richmond's "Lebanese Mafia." According to assistant U.S. attorney N. George Metcalf, three immigrant clans were involved in everything from theft to gambling. Their leaders were all violent, but none more so—or more dan-

Leo Joseph Koury

gerous or clever—than the Lebanese Mafia's unofficial godfather, Leo Joseph Koury.

Leo Koury was born in Pittsburgh, Pennsylvania. His father, Joseph N. Koury, later brought his oldest son and the rest of the family to the Richmond area. Then Joseph Koury deserted Leo's mother and the children and returned to his native Lebanon.

The fatherless boy matured into a burly, curly-haired young adult with a weakness for poker (at which he reputedly was peerless in Virginia) as well as other avenues to a fast buck. Leo was arrested for the first time in 1954, at age twenty, for stealing auto parts. But Koury also built himself a facade of respectability. He married a local girl and fathered four children by her. He established a number of legitimate enterprises, from restaurants to apartment complexes. Every summer he umpired amateur softball games. Leo even joined the American Legion.

At heart, however, Leo Koury was—or is—a mean-tempered hood with a talent for manipulating others and a flair for plotting. "He looked like a sleazy businessman," says George Metcalf. "And Leo invented some really novel ways of doing business."

One of his innovations was insurance fraud. "Leo," says FBI agent Chuck Evans, "hired guys to get into phony car accidents in parking lots. They'd go get a couple old cars and run into each other. Then they'd grab their necks and head for the hospital. Later, there'd be an insurance settlement and Leo would take his cut."

Koury's schemes did not always work out. Once, he and his band of gunsels tried to torch a house in the Richmond area. As prosecutor Metcalf tells the story, the gang sloshed too much gasoline around inside the residence, so that its rooms filled with fumes. When Leo then chucked a lit Molotov cocktail through one of the windows, the trapped vapors exploded in a flameless *puff!* that blew out the windows but left the rest of the structure undamaged.

Such mistakes were rare for Leo, and when he did make a misstep, he was always canny enough to avoid jail time. In 1964, for instance, charges against him for possessing stolen merchandise were dropped. Likewise, forgery and drug-possession allegations were later dismissed.

"He would lead people to believe that he was immune from prosecution," says prosecutor Metcalf, "because he had friends in high places. And he always had a lot of money. Therefore, he had credibility. People were willing to do things with, and for, him. And they didn't give a damn what he wanted done."

Beginning in the late 1960s, Koury pioneered the exploitation of Richmond's homosexual community by opening several immensely profitable gay bars and after-hours clubs around town. All Leo's joints were low-lit, seedy and overcharged for drinks, a profit formula that inevitably attracted unwelcome emulators.

In February of 1975, an entrepreneur named Wayne Cash opened his own Cha-Cha Club downtown. Mindful of Koury's reputation, Cash also hired some muscle in the person of Chuck Kernaghan, a local tough who went to work for Cash as his bouncer.

Koury first tried to intimidate Cash by sending a trio of goons into the Cha-Cha Club to bust up the place. "Then I think Chuck Kernaghan got in his face," says Metcalf. Whatever Koury's reason for wanting Kernaghan out of the way, Wayne Cash's bouncer vanished that spring.

At this juncture FBI agent Evans entered the picture. Evans had been helping to search for Tommy Gandolfo, a fugitive bank robber from South Carolina. A phone tap revealed that Gandolfo's girlfriend in South Carolina had recently called a Richmond telephone number. When Chuck Evans was asked to check out whoever she was trying to reach, he discovered she had called a pay phone at one of Leo Koury's bars.

"I took Tommy's picture over and showed it

to Leo," remembers agent Evans. "Leo says, 'Oh sure, that's Tommy Gandolfo. Haven't seen him in three or four years.' Blah, blah, blah. 'Like to help ya.' Then he pats me on the back and sends me on my way.

"Just as I'm walking out of the parking lot I see someone pull up in Leo's Cadillac. He stopped at the curb and I looked. It was Tommy Gandolfo! So I walked up to Tommy and grabbed him and took him down and locked him up."

Gandolfo felt no particular loyalty to Koury. So, in an effort to reduce his prison time, he began to sing. "Tommy said, 'Myself and a couple other guys dumped this Chuck Kernaghan,'" agent Evans remembers. "Then he relayed how Leo sort of suckered Kernaghan into coming over to Leo's house. When Kernaghan walked into the living room, [another member of Koury's gang] let him have it with a .38. They wrapped him up in a carpet, put him in a locker and then they tied him down with chains and a car bumper and took him out to the Rappahannock River. They used a boat owned by a guy named Butch Walton to deep-six Kernaghan."

Gandolfo also had other news to share. He told Chuck Evans that within the next couple days Leo Koury and his bunch intended to kidnap and hold for ransom E. Claiborne Robins, Jr., president of the Richmond-based A. H. Robins Co., the makers of Robitussin cough syrup among other well-known products. The FBI was able to warn Robins in time and spirited the alarmed executive out of town before Koury could pounce.

In January 1977, according to the FBI, Koury

dispatched one of his goons to shoot up a rival bar called the Male Box. One patron was killed and two others injured. The Male Box closed a few days later.

Brutal as he was toward his competitors, Leo did sometimes welcome outside investments in his own gay bars. But these business partners soon discovered that working with Leo Koury could be even more dangerous than competing against him. In a typical $40,000 bar investment deal, the contract would call for $10,000 down, $10,000 more in six months and the balance over a number of years. The papers specifically stated that if Leo's partners failed to make a payment, or if they died, their share in the bar would revert to him.

These terms explain why one such partner was deeply frightened one day to discover Koury's associate, Eddy Loehr, lurking near his house wearing a ski mask and packing a gun. The man thought that Leo had marked him for erasure.

Eddy Loehr immediately became a priority subject for the Bureau, which hoped to turn him (before he completed his assignment) the way they had turned Tommy Gandolfo. Agents dug hard into Loehr's background and found they could link him to at least one unsolved bank robbery. The FBI also learned that Loehr's girlfriend was a call girl known professionally as "Kitten." Late one night, "Kitten" was summoned by telephone to a Richmond motel, where she no doubt expected to find the usual drunk businessman. Instead, she was met by a team of agents. "We just sat her down and told her the facts of life," says Chuck Evans. "She gushed up everything she knew about Eddy, including the fact that he'd done this bank robbery and that Leo had hired him to kill this other guy."

Next, the FBI approached Loehr himself with their evidence. He, like Tommy Gandolfo, agreed to help the Bureau build its case against Leo Koury. Eddy Loehr wore a tape recorder to several meetings with Koury over the coming months.

By the autumn of 1978, the FBI's investigation was nearly complete. Assistant U.S. attorney N. George Metcalf was about to file the first of two federal indictments, and local prosecutors were preparing charges against Koury. Altogether, he would be accused of racketeering, murder, attempted murder, extortion, mail fraud and obstruction of justice.

The preparations were made in secret, but it was no secret to Leo Koury that time was getting tight for him. "He sort of started to figure that the jig was up," explains agent Evans. "His friends had started acting weird. Leo knew that this person and that person had been before the grand jury. Eddy Loehr started avoiding him. Leo figured, 'Oh-oh, they're gonna get me. I better take off.'"

And that is just what Leo Koury did. In October of 1978 he reportedly grabbed a couple suitcases full of cash—and a girlfriend—and drove off in his Cadillac. The following year, he was spotted in São Paulo, Brazil, where he has relatives and where he apparently worked for a time teaching English. Otherwise, the FBI knows nothing for a certainty about Leo Joseph Koury's whereabouts for the past twelve years.

He is the senior member of the Bureau's "Ten Most Wanted" List.

"It looks like he's just fallen off the end of the earth," says agent Henry Handy, who is now in charge of the Koury investigation. Handy is the twelfth agent to take over the case since 1978.

Few people in the Richmond area lament Leo Joseph Koury's disappearance. "I don't want to talk about Leo anymore," his wife, Jeanette, told a reporter in 1988. "Life has been a lot calmer since he left."

The FBI, on the other hand, is very eager to see Leo Koury again, even though there is no longer much realistic hope that he can be successfully tried and convicted for all his alleged crimes. The statute of limitations has run out on many cases, while others, including the murder raps, have grown so old that the chances of a successful prosecution have dimmed considerably. What is more, the FBI has spent a considerable amount of time and money trying to catch Leo Koury, exhausting every lead and strategy, including a computer enhancement of his mug shot to suggest what he might look like today. Nothing, as yet, has worked, and the FBI is embarrassed by its continued failure.

As a result, the feds now reluctantly concede that they are ready to negotiate some sort of bargain if Koury will come in on his own. "I think," says agent Jack Colwell, "that we could sit down with Leo and work out something mutually equitable."

"Yeah," prosecutor Metcalf agrees with a sardonic chuckle, "tell Leo, 'Come home! All is forgiven.'"

4. "Street Punk"

ROBERT EARL JONES
Nashville, Tennessee

DATE OF BIRTH: SOMETIME IN 1958
HEIGHT: FIVE FEET, FIVE INCHES
WEIGHT: 141 POUNDS
HAIR: BLACK
EYES: BROWN
DISTINGUISHING MARKS OR SCARS: "BARBO" TATTOOED ON
  LEFT HAND AT WRIST
ALSO KNOWN AS: WILL KIRKPATRICK
REWARD: $1,000 FROM NASHVILLE CRIMESTOPPERS
         (615) 74-CRIME
CONTACT: NASHVILLE, TENNESSEE METRO POLICE
         MURDER SQUAD
         (615) 862-7329

"He's just one of your typical little street punks that sell dope," says Nashville metro police homicide detective Grady Elam of Robert ("Buck") Jones, who is wanted for the 1982 murder of David Milsap.

This is how the crime occurred:

On Tuesday night, June 15, 1982, David Milsap took his girlfriend to a Nashville Sounds (AAA professional) baseball game. "And on his way home," says Detective Elam, "Milsap de-

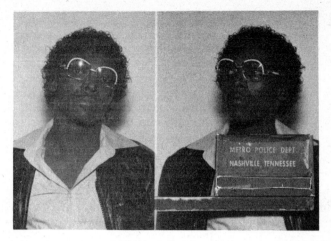

Robert Earl Jones

cided to stop by and get himself a little grass to smoke."

The "stop by" site was the corner of Sylvan and Eighth streets, an open-air drug market in a largely black section of Nashville. "It's a bad area," according to Grady Elam. "We've had *numerous* killings over there in the past several years."

Milsap was aware of the possible peril. He left his girlfriend at a Bi-Rite supermarket on South Sixth Street and told her to wait inside, where she'd be safe until he returned with his dope. That was the last she saw of her boyfriend alive.

A few minutes later, Milsap drove up to the intersection where he expected to see the usual group of four or five dealers. It was first come, first served, so at the sight of a customer the dealers usually raced to get to his car door first. This night, however, Buck Jones came to the driver's side window with a gun in his hand. Police surmise that Milsap either tried to grab the gun away or he tried to drive off. Whatever occurred, the handgun discharged a single bullet that killed David Milsap where he sat.

For homicides of this sort, where a suspect is not immediately identified, there is a special "Murder Squad" within the Nashville metro police. This group of detectives, including Grady Elam, maintains extensive contacts inside Nashville's illicit drug culture. It was not more than a few days before the Murder Squad's snitches reported back that Buck Jones was the drug dealer who shot David Milsap. Within a couple weeks the detectives had narrowed their hunt to an apartment leased to Jones's cousin, where they arrested the suspect.

Unfortunately, Robert Earl Jones did not remain in custody for long. As Detective Elam recalls, on the way to his arraignment Jones broke loose from his deputy sheriff escorts and ran away. He has not been recaptured.

At first, says Elam, Jones probably hid out among his friends and relatives in Franklin, Tennessee, about twenty-five miles southwest of Nashville. Recently, however, he has been bold enough to show his face in Nashville again. In fact, he participated in an armed robbery, was identified by a witness and is now wanted for that crime as well as for his escape and for the murder of David Milsap.

5. Escape Artist

THERESA MARIE GROSSO
Baltimore, Maryland

DATE OF BIRTH: MARCH 13, 1948
HEIGHT: FIVE FEET, FIVE INCHES
WEIGHT: 135 POUNDS (APPROX.)
HAIR: USUALLY BLACK OR BROWN
EYES: HAZEL
DISTINGUISHING MARKS OR SCARS: SCAR ON NECK AND SUPERFICIAL RAZOR-AND-GLASS-CUT SCARS ON BOTH WRISTS FROM ATTEMPTED SUICIDE
ALSO KNOWN AS: BERTHA THERESA KEENE, PATRICIA ANN LENO, ANITA PALM, ANITA LYNCH, ANTOINETTE WEST, THERESA MARIE KEENE.
REWARD: NONE
CONTACT: CORPORAL GLORIA MCNAIR
              MARYLAND STATE POLICE
              FUGITIVE APPREHENSION UNIT
              (301) 653-4406

On Friday night, September 26, 1969, twenty-one-year-old Theresa Grosso of Baltimore went out partying with two friends, a loan-company cashier and a dancer at the Two O'Clock Club on Greenmount Avenue in Baltimore. Evidently, all three women were drunk by midnight.

That is what witnesses told police, according

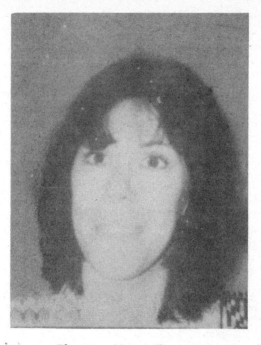

Theresa Marie Grosso

to the Sunday, September 28, editions of the Baltimore *Sun*. These people recounted seeing the three friends in front of Judge's Musical Lounge on Greenmount (not far from where Theresa's dancer friend worked) shortly past midnight. They also told how the doorman, twenty-eight-year-old Melvin Nicholas Luckhart, demanded to see proof of age before he would allow the inebriated threesome inside.

Harsh words were exchanged. Then—still according to these witnesses—Theresa Grosso produced a .25-caliber pistol from her purse and fired a point-blank round into Luckart's chest. The doorman collapsed and expired on the pavement.

Several onlookers grabbed one of Grosso's friends as Theresa and the other woman fled by car, which witnesses were able to describe in detail to the police. Later that morning, Theresa Marie Grosso was arrested at her residence and booked for first-degree murder. Bond was denied.

A year later, Ms. Grosso was convicted of Melvin Luckart's murder. A Baltimore court sentenced her to spend the balance of her natural life at the Maryland Correctional Facility for Women in Jessup.

Theresa Grosso, however, had other ideas.

Despair over her incarceration may have led Theresa to attempt suicide by slitting her wrists at Jessup. Or the self-inflicted wounds might have been part of a ruse. Authorities at the prison aren't certain. But they do know that Ms. Grosso was always ready to run.

She engineered her first escape on February 13, 1971. She was loose for eleven days before her recapture, by U.S. marshals, in Washington, D.C. Next, Theresa and an accomplice slipped away on July 14, 1972, but were caught just hours later by the Maryland State Police.

The third time she went over the fence was March 3, 1976. On this occasion Theresa Grosso remained at large for fifteen months, until June of 1977, when FBI agents apprehended her in Miami. During this period of freedom, she apparently made the acquaintance of William

Palm, a 180-pound, five-foot, eight-inch white male with blue eyes and brown hair.

The Maryland State Police have charged Bill Palm with aiding Theresa Grosso in her next and last—and so far successful—escape try on August 29, 1979. That evening, she and a friend at the correctional facility fashioned dummies in their bunks from stuffed sweaters and other clothes. Then they cut a rectangular hole in the screen over their window and descended to freedom via a bedsheet rope.

Nothing is known of Grosso and William Palm's whereabouts until about two years later when the couple showed up in Ashford, Alabama, which appears in AAA road maps as a tiny white bead on U.S. Route 84, a slender red thread that snakes across from Dothan, Alabama, about ten miles west of Ashford, and wends another ten miles or so to the Chattahoochee River and the extreme southwestern corner of Georgia. The north Florida border is but twenty miles away.

Grosso and Palm, calling themselves Patricia and William Leno, arrived in Ashford driving a Ford U-Haul truck. They rented a house trailer and set about earning a living by doing odd jobs for local residents.

They were careful not to call attention to themselves and lived quietly in Ashford until February 6, 1982. Around noon that day, Grosso and Palm drove their U-Haul up Route 84 to Dothan and headed for a shopping district, where they found an Albertson's supermarket.

Theresa and Bill expected to do a little shoplifting.

They strolled into the Albertson's with an infant girl (parentage unknown) and headed for the produce section. Unfortunately for the couple's plans, however, store manager David Jerry and one of his employees, George Faulkner, watched intently as Theresa boosted $8.54 worth of grapes. Then she grabbed a $3.59 box of Sun Giant whole dates and two cans of glossy-white enamel spray paint, which sold for $3.19 apiece. Grosso tucked the stolen merchandise into a large brown shoulder bag, and walked nonchalantly to front of the store with Palm, who was carrying the child. At the door, both suspects took off at a sprint. Messrs. Jerry and Faulkner ran after them.

Palm split off with the baby, heading across the street into a Piggly Wiggly store parking lot. Grosso quickly jettisoned her bulky brown bag, which enabled her to outrun her pursuers. Jerry and Faulkner finally gave up the chase and returned to Albertson's, where they telephoned the police.

Meanwhile, Theresa Grosso also found a phone and dialed the man and wife who were her and Palm's landlords in Ashford. She told them that the U-Haul had broken down and asked if they would come to pick up their stranded tenants, the Lenos. The landlords said yes.

The first cop on the scene was Billy Gilmer. Officer Gilmer, who subsequently left the Dothan police and opened a seafood restaurant called Gilmo's, remembers today that he found William Palm—a.k.a. William Leno—in the Piggly Wiggly lot with the Ford U-Haul and the little girl. Something about the truck and Leno's appearance seemed very familiar to him, but Gilmer couldn't quite place where he'd seen the suspect. He questioned Leno, who could produce no identification. Leno also denied that he knew the woman shoplifter with whom he'd fled the Albertson's.

According to Gilmer, he interrogated Leno just before the Dothan Police Department's 2:00 P.M. shift change. He says that the corporal above him in the department did not want to be bothered processing a "penny ante" suspected shoplifter when he could be at home instead. So the corporal ordered Gilmer to let Mr. Leno loose.

At about the same time, the Lenos' landlords arrived in Dothan from Ashford. They picked up Theresa Grosso—the woman they knew as Patricia Leno—and began to drive slowly through the shopping district, looking for her husband.

So far, it had not been Theresa Grosso's day. Now the situation turned decidedly dicier for her. Officer Billy Gilmer was personally acquainted with her landlords and recognized their family sedan as he was driving his squad car back to the station that afternoon. Worse still, in a hardly-to-be-believed coincidence, Officer Gilmer also recognized Ms. Grosso (who was partially disguised behind a pair of eyeglasses) in the backseat.

As he explains the incident, Gilmer at the time was commuting down to Ashford each weekend to help his cousin build a house. He distinctly recalled several occasions when he would look out across the road from the building site in Ashford and see a U-Haul truck and a man and a woman picking up windfall pecans.

Theresa and Bill.

When Gilmer saw Grosso that afternoon, he suddenly put two and two together. He stopped his friends' car and explained that their passenger was a suspected thief. Gilmer took the handcuffed and sobbing Theresa Grosso back to Albertson's to be identified. Then, at the police station, she was booked as Patricia Leno (Grosso produced an apparently valid passport under that name) and charged with third-degree theft of property, a misdemeanor.

Officer Gilmer, of course, had no idea that he had collared a notorious escape artist and fugitive murderess from Maryland; he wouldn't know Patricia Leno's true identity until an FBI man came around several days later. It was a rueful visit, because by then the prize had long since been lost. Just hours after her arrest—and unbeknownst to Gilmer—Theresa Maria Grosso snookered a local bondsman into standing her $500 bail. By midnight, less than twelve hours after the failed shoplifting expedition at Albertson's, the Grosso/Palm/Lenos of Ashford, Alabama, had vanished entirely.

They have not been seen since.

6. Smuggler

GERALD LYLE HEMP
Palm Beach, Florida

DATE OF BIRTH: SEPTEMBER 5, 1934
HEIGHT: FIVE FEET, ELEVEN INCHES
WEIGHT: 220 POUNDS
HAIR: BROWN, RECEDING
EYES: BLUE
DISTINGUISHING MARKS OR SCARS: ONE-INCH SCAR ON RIGHT SIDE OF RIGHT EYE. TATTOOS: ''AIRBORNE RANGER'' ON UPPER LEFT ARM, A GEISHA ON HIS LEFT FOREARM, AND A ROSE ON HIS RIGHT ARM.
ALSO KNOWN AS: GEORGE BAKER, RONALD CARLSON, JAMES COMSTOCK, ALAN EDWARD KIMBALL, ELBERT MAXWELL MORAN, JR. AND JERRY WHITTIER
REWARD: NONE
CONTACT: UNITED STATES MARSHALS COMMUNICATION CENTER
(800) 336-0102

Gerald Hemp's life of crime dates back at least as far as 1965 when the Peoria, Illinois, native was convicted in California of first-degree robbery. He received a sentence of five years to life. In the joint, Hemp studied hard and taught himself to become a master electrician. But he is foremost a felon, and dope smuggling is the aptly-named Mr. Hemp's forte. In the course of

Gerald Lyle Hemp

becoming a major cocaine importer, say authorities, Gerald Hemp also has had a hand in as many as eight murders. He is a suspect in three of these killings.

The first of the murders occurred in November of 1981. The victim was an unidentified man found dead near the Atlantic airport. The most recent killing that the U.S. marshals will discuss is that of an Alexandria, Virginia, pediatrician, Dr. Robert Rixie, who was murdered in September of 1984. A close friend of Hemp's has been convicted for the Rixie homicide. Then there is the death of Charles L. Kagler, Sr., about which much more is known. Kagler was Hemp's drug-running partner until their business and personal relationship began to sour.

Hemp and Kagler were both pilots, although only Kagler was licensed to fly. Beginning in 1979 or 1980, they operated a high-volume and extremely lucrative cocaine-smuggling business, flying hundreds and hundreds of pounds of the white powder north from Columbia to drop points in the United States. Their enormous profits financed a lavish life-style for Hemp, but it was not too long after they started getting rich that the partners' luck started running out.

In March of 1981, authorities in Tennessee seized 619 pounds of Hemp–Kagler cocaine— reportedly worth more than $200 million—just arrived by air from South America. The raid remains the record cocaine bust in Tennessee. Shortly thereafter, Hemp and Kagler lost another 369 pounds of coke in an abortive operation near the town of Mossyhead on the Florida panhandle. Kagler himself was in the pilot's seat. As he landed the plane, he saw customs agents running toward it. He jumped out of the cockpit ahead of them, and darted to safety in the bushes, breaking his wrist in the process. A short while later, the partners were deprived of yet one more shipment in a raid at Marco Island, Florida.

The string of misadventures told on their

nerves and their partnership. For a while Kagler struck out on his own. Then, according to federal officials, the partners agreed to rejoin forces for one last big operation. That, at least, is what Charlie Kagler thought he was getting into.

The plan called for him to fly down to Colombia to pick up the coke. But as Kagler brought his plane down to a remote jungle landing strip, gunfire broke out from all sides. Somehow, he managed to land the aircraft and then escaped into the Colombian jungle. Charlie hid out for a couple weeks before making his way to Freeport in the Bahamas.

This was in early June 1982. Kagler surmised that his erstwhile friend, Gerry Hemp, was behind the murder attempt. After returning to the United States, he told several of their mutual acquaintances and associates of his suspicions. On June 21, Charlie disappeared from his residence near Palm Beach. Nine days later the police fished his bloated corpse out of the Florida surf. He had sustained massive head injuries, and the cops at first guessed someone had run over him with a powerboat. An autopsy, however, established the cause of death was a gunshot wound.

Gerald Hemp, who at the time resided under one of his many aliases in a posh Fort Lauderdale condominium nearby, was in Panama the day Charlie Kagler's remains were retrieved. He stayed outside the United States until September 30, 1982, when he hazarded a return to Ft. Lauderdale. There he was arrested, not for the Kagler slaying, but in connection with the Tennessee cocaine bust of the previous year. The following January 1983, Gerald Hemp was convicted on four counts in a Tennessee courtroom and received four ten-year prison sentences to be served consecutively.

Then—and suddenly—Hemp's losing streak was over. First, his attorney arranged for him to do his time in Florida, a more congenial climate for Hemp. Second, through what U.S. Marshal Mike Earp in Tallahassee describes as a "clerical error," Hemp's consecutive sentences handed down in Tennessee became "concurrent" in Florida, meaning he could be eligible for release in a relatively short time. Third, the state of Florida had just then launched a major project to upgrade the electrical wiring in its prison system. What serendipity that the new man from Tennessee, Gerry Hemp, was an expert around electrical equipment?

Over the coming months, Hemp was moved six or seven times as he toured Florida's prisons, improving their wiring. The security at each new facility was progressively more minimal until he landed at Lantana, near Palm Beach. On June 9, 1984, he received a visit from a person described by prison personnel as "an exotic-looking Oriental female" of unknown name or connection to Hemp. The U.S. marshals now know her as "the visitor from Tokyo." The following day Gerald, unescorted by any prison personnel, was allowed out of the facility to keep a dental appointment. He never returned.

Since then, the authorities have received hundreds of tips as to Gerald Hemp's possible whereabouts, but none have led anywhere.

Hemp is reputedly a master of disguise. Federal lawmen assume he has rejoined Florida's drug underground—"Hemp has ties and associations all over Florida," says Marshal Earp, "and obviously he likes it here"—but they recognize that he is crafty and well connected enough to be anywhere in the world. After more than six years of fruitless searching, they know they are going to have to get lucky to catch him.

7. Eight Ball

WILLIE JAMES BUCHANAN
Nashville, Tennessee

DATE OF BIRTH: SOME TIME IN 1948 OR 1949
HEIGHT: SIX FEET, THREE INCHES
WEIGHT: 193 POUNDS
HAIR: BLACK
EYES: BROWN
ALSO KNOWN AS: CHUBBY
REWARD: $1,000 FROM NASHVILLE CRIMESTOPPERS
(615) 74-CRIME
CONTACT: NASHVILLE METRO POLICE
        MURDER SQUAD
        (615) 862-7329

The fund of available information on Willie James Buchanan is meager. "Chubby," as he was known around Nashville, usually could be found hanging out at the Last Chance, a liquor store in East Nashville. He may have been born in Shelbyville, Tennessee. His rap sheet shows arrests for petit larceny, shoplifting and passing bad checks, but no charges of assaultive or violent behavior ever were filed against him.

In the summer of 1987 Buchanan was friendly with Joe Louis Hodge, then forty-nine, a stoutly built former bricklayer known for his prowess as a pool player. One night at the Club Sexual

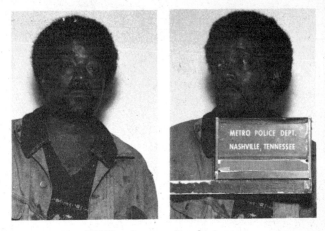

Willie James Buchanan

Healing on JoJohnston Street, Chubby and Joe decided on a game of eight ball. According to what his girlfriend, Helen Bradley, later recalled, Joe suggested a special rule, a test of skill. The final, winning shot, Hodge proposed, had to be banked in off a pool-table rail, or it wouldn't count. Chubby seemed to agree, but when Buchanan had a chance to put in the winning eight ball, he shot it straight and claimed victory.

Chubby's disdain for the rules upset Joe Louis Hodge. Words were exchanged. A wrestling match ensued. Other patrons broke up the fight. No report of the fracas was made to the police. As far as anyone knows, there were no further hostilities, physical or otherwise, between Buchanan and the older man.

Then came the chilly night of February 9, 1988. Chubby and Joe's circle of friends enjoyed evenings gathering together in the vacant lot behind Jay's liquor store, also on Jo-Johnston Street. They'd get some wine and then, for warmth, the group would start a fire in a big barrel. "They just hung out at this barrel," explains Detective Mike Smith of the Nashville Police's Murder Squad. "It was their socializing place."

At about 8:00 P.M., according to witnesses, about half a dozen people were at the barrel, including Joe Hodge, who was sitting down, and his girlfriend, Helen Bradley, who was standing next to him. Next to Helen stood Chubby Buchanan, who did not behave in any strange or belligerent way toward Joe Hodge, except that the two men did not exchange a word or glance.

Then, with no word or warning, Chubby whirled around, pulled out a large-caliber pistol and started shooting at Joe. He fired several rounds. One bullet hit Hodge in the chest. Hodge was later pronounced dead at Nashville's Baptist Hospital.

Chubby Buchanan remains at large, and Detective Smith concedes that he has no idea where his suspect might be. As for the apparent banality of Joe Hodge's death—a bloody murder by a suspect with a trivial motive and no history of violent behavior—Mike Smith shrugs the homicide detective's shrug. "That happens," he explains. "I had a couple of guys one time—seventy-two and seventy-three years old. They got in a fight over a checker game. And one of them pulled a knife and stabbed the other one *twenty-seven times*!"

8. The Trestle Murder

PAUL DAVID CREWS
Bartow, Florida

DATE OF BIRTH: AUGUST 2, 1952
HEIGHT: FIVE FEET, FIVE INCHES
WEIGHT: 150 POUNDS
HAIR: BROWN
EYES: BLUE
DISTINGUISHING MARKS OR SCARS: SCAR ON LEFT THUMB AND PALM; SCARS ABOVE BOTH NIPPLES; MOLE ON LEFT CHEEK; THE LETTER "C" TATTOOS ON LEFT SHOULDER, "CASEY" TATTOOED ON RIGHT SHOULDER
ALSO KNOWN AS: DAVID, DAVIE
REWARD: $1,000 FROM CRIMESTOPPERS
CONTACT: FLORIDA'S MOST WANTED FUGITIVES
(800) 342-7768 (INSIDE FLORIDA)
OR
(904) 487-0932

The few residents of mid-peninsular Bartow, Florida, who bothered to notice migrant fruit-picker Paul David Crews remember him as snakes-in-the-head strange. First, there were the tattoos and those bizarre scars on his chest, which looked like souvenirs from some sort of primitive mortification rite. Then there was his life-style. The South Carolina native lived in a lean-to under a railroad trestle. When he wasn't

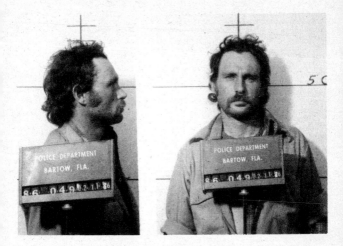

Paul David Crews

resting there on his mattress or lawn chair, Crews could usually be found fishing in the nearby Peace River. Evenings and Saturdays he went to the local public library to read science fiction and the latest best-sellers. "He smoked," remembered a library staffer to reporter Martha Bowman of the Polk County *Democrat*, "but never got up, not even to go to the bathroom or to get water."

Paul David Crews wasn't suspected of being much more than weird, however, until Wednesday night, July 2, 1986. That evening, witnesses reported, Crews went to a beer joint and dance hall called Madge's Bar on U.S. Route 17, north of Bartow. Clemmie J. Arnold, fifty-six, of Bartow was in Madge's that night as well. Crews and Arnold met, talked and, at about 1:45 A.M., they left together. Witnesses reported that Paul David asked Clemmie for a ride home to his trestle.

Late the next afternoon, two fishermen found Ms. Arnold's corpse in some high weeds about 500 feet from Paul David's primitive lair. Her throat was slashed six times, and although Clemmie had not been sexually assaulted, her clothes had been cut from her body and were found in a pile nearby. Ms. Arnold's maroon and white 1983 Oldsmobile Cutlass was missing, and so was Paul David Crews.

At eight o'clock on the night of the third he was positively identified in Cleveland County, North Carolina, where his brother, Ray Horne, lived. A gas-station attendant placed Crews in Arnold's Olds, and reported that both the back-seat of the car and the five-dollar bill with which Crews bought gas were bloodstained.

The Cleveland County sheriff was notified, and a patrol car was sent to the Horne residence. "While the deputy waited for assistance," reported the *Democrat*, "Crews and his brother ran from the home and jumped into the car and drove away."

Paul David eluded his police pursuers; Clemmie Arnold's blood-splattered Olds was recovered two miles away. The next day, July 4, Crews was reported seen again, afoot, on one of Cleveland County's back roads. Then an anonymous caller directed the police to a mountain hunter's cabin where Crews apparently was hiding out. Searchers found traces of their quarry—sandwich wrappers, bloody rags, money, a cigarette lighter and a half-drunk can of beer, still cool—but Paul David Crews himself had melted back into the forest. His trail then went cold.

Since then, the alleged murderer has from time to time been seen back in the Bartow region, most recently in the autumn of 1989. He was placed on the Florida Department of Law Enforcement's "Ten Most Wanted" list in January of 1990.

SERIAL KILLERS

There is no category of modern murderer that provokes greater horror than serial, or pattern, killers. Those who so far have been captured—David Berkowitz, Ted Bundy, John Gacy, Wayne Williams and the like—are among the most notorious crime figures of the past two decades. The cases that remain open—that of Green River in the northwest, of San Diego, the Zodiac slayings in northern California and others—continue to haunt dozens of American communities.

The public dread of serial murderers derives in part from the unseen, lurking menace they pose to victim classes, usually women and children. A serial killer is a predator who strikes anywhere, without warning. Another potent source of fear is knowledge of how these men behave once victims are within their power. Bundy, for example, revealed just before his execution in 1989 that he dismembered some victims, decapitated others, committed necrophilia and played bizarre psychological tricks on the girls he hunted. A recent arrestee in Delaware allegedly used pliers to pinch and squeeze his female victims' breasts and noses. In Alaska, serial slayer Robert Chris Hansen kidnapped prostitutes and flew them out into the wilderness in his private airplane. Alone in the back country, Hansen later explained to police, he stripped the women, released them and then hunted them down with his big-game rifle.

The frightfulness of such episodes is plain, but gauging the threat posed by serial killers to society in general is difficult. FBI special agent John Douglas, head of the Bureau's newly named "Investigative and Operational Support Unit" within the National Center for the Analysis of Violent Crimes at Quantico, Virginia, says the actual number of active serial killers cannot be known, but may be inferred from available statistics.

Douglas points out that thirteen to fifteen serial killers are captured and brought to trial each year in the United States. The second statistic of interest, he says, is the solution rate for murder in the United States, where about 20,000 people a year are reported as homicide victims. Since the late 1960s, the murder solution rate has dropped from about 90 percent to roughly 70 percent; about 5,000 to 6,000 reported murders now go unsolved each year. "We cannot say that is based solely on serial killers," explains Douglas, "but serial killers are certainly contributing to that number."

There are also the much more nebulous missing persons' lists. It is likely that a significant number of these people become murder victims too—perhaps serial murder victims. And there is the other broad class of potential serial murder victims, the untold thousands of discarded or runaway children whose names may never appear on any official list, even in death. Most police agencies of any size have at least one set of unidentified bones or other human remains in their custody.

If pressed to make a guess, agent Douglas says the FBI feels that there are about forty serial killers who are actively murdering victims at any one time. Their most common target: prostitutes.

The newspaper *USA Today* published an intriguing roster in mid-March of 1990. According to the paper, since 1988 there have been ten unsolved prostitute murders in Washington, D.C., six in Kansas City (where a suspect has been taken into custody), sixteen more in Rochester, New York (where a suspect also has been arrested), thirty-one in Miami, ten in Tampa, a dozen in Los Angeles and forty-two in San Diego.

Why so many hookers? "They're just easy victims," Douglas believes. "I mean, you don't have to be a Don Juan or use any kind of sophisticated ruse or con like a Ted Bundy did to get to a potential victim. With prostitutes, they're the ones [who must provide] the line or the ruse to convince a guy to pay for their services. And there are so many of them out there. They become the ideal victim."

Do prostitutes, as a class, have specific psychological significance to these men? "You have to analyze the case to determine how they were killed," Douglas replies. "In some prostitute murders you see a quick kill; in others, there could be an element of torture involved. The primary thing, really, is punishment, anger, manipulation—*domination* of that victim. If he has the time and the right resources, such as a vehicle where he can tie up the victim, he'd like to spend some time in carrying out the punishment."

But agent Douglas cautions against overemphasizing the prostitute's calling or station in life in analyzing why they so often are a serial killer's victim of choice. "It's just that they are readily available," he says. "These guys won't pass up someone who is hitchhiking along the highway. It's just an opportunistic type of thing."

The largest and so-far unsolved serial murder case anywhere is that of the forty-nine females, mostly prostitutes, who were slain, mostly by strangulation, by the Green River killer or killers in the northwest between July of 1982 and March of 1984. Ordinarily, about twenty or twenty-one people are murdered each month in Washington State, so that the Green River killings committed there represented a greater-than-10-percent rise in the state's homicide rate for the period.

The first five Green River victims were found soon after the killings started, and it was from their discovery in and along the Green River just south of Seattle near Kent, Washington, that the case received its name. King County police captain Robert Evans, the former head of the so-called Green River Task Force, says that the first group of remains, found in July and August of 1982, were the only ones dumped (carefully weighted with stones) in or near the river. One theory of the case is that these five were the *only* victims of the original Green River Killer, and that the other forty-four dead women are the work of one, or perhaps two, other predatory males.

Copycat killing, or murder inspired by example, are both phenomena well known to homicide investigators. What is more, serial killers are especial students of one another's work, always honing and refining their techniques.

Robert Keppel, chief investigator for the Washington State attorney general and a former King County (Seattle) detective who headed up the task-force hunt for Ted Bundy in the 1970s, has consulted on the Green River case. He notes that the killer or killers became increasingly sophisticated over time, a pattern consistent with other serial murder cases.

"Originally," says Keppel, "the bodies were found within five miles of where the victims disappeared. Later, they were recovered 50 to 190 miles away and were basically scattered remains. We know the Green River killer has buried bodies. We know he has put them out in remote areas. We know he has covered them up with twigs and bushes. We know he has put them in the river and held them down [to make them sink]. All that sort of stuff. That is quite an effort to make sure people aren't found."

The Seattle and King County police, together with the Washington State Patrol, have spent more than $10 million on the Green River investigation. At one time as many as fifty-six policemen with fourteen support personnel and a dozen FBI agents were working on the case. In all, the task force has received 20,000 tips and checked out 1,450 suspects. In the process several crimes unconnected to the Green River killings have been solved, and several serial killers have been arrested and charged—but not the Green River killer himself, or themselves.

It appeared for a while in 1989 that the case had finally been broken with the arrest of William J. Stevens II, a thirty-eight-year-old former law student (like Ted Bundy) and convicted burglar. The police called Stevens a "viable suspect" for some weeks. Here are some of the reasons why:

—One theory of the Green River case is that the killer posed as a cop when approaching his prostitute victims. A search of Stevens's house disclosed a collection of police badges and uniforms, plus radios, handcuffs and other cop paraphernalia. The search also uncovered a hidden room into which Stevens allegedly admitted bringing prostitutes from time to time.

—Victim Denise Darcel Bush, last seen alive near Sea-Tac airport on October 2, 1982, was later found dead in Tigard, Oregon. Stevens's gas receipts place him in Tigard on October 3, 5, 8 and 11 of that year.

—Trina Hunter, another victim, vanished from Seattle on Christmas Eve, 1982. That same day Stevens bought gas to the south in Clark County, where Trina Hunter's remains eventually were uncovered.

—An Oregon prostitute named Kimberly Yvette Hill was last seen alive in Portland on October 26, 1984. Police later established that Stevens placed long-distance telephone calls from Portland on the twenty-fifth and twenty-sixth.

Suspects have been convicted—and executed—on flimsier evidence than this, yet William Jay Stevens will not be arrested or tried for the Green River killings because of unequivocal evidence that he is innocent. Despite all the tantalizing coincidences, they remain just that, coincidences.

"Those things always hurt," says retired Los Angeles police detective Pierce R. Brooks of the disappointment the Seattle authorities experienced when it turned out that William Stevens could not have committed the killings. Brooks, an authority on serial killers who has also advised the police in the Green River case, opines that from what he knows of the investigation, "It's gonna be a tough case unless somebody is caught driving with a body in his car or someone walks in and say, 'I did it. I'm the Green River guy.' "

The chances of that happening are remote. "Because of all the publicity," says Brooks, "serial killers are much more learned today then they were ten years ago. I'm not criticizing. That's just the way it is. And as you know, they have a tremendous personality disorder. It is their way of life and it is something they cannot change.

"I've talked to serial killers and they tell me, 'Hey, there's no way I'm gonna change, pal!' I've [also] seen a letter from a killer, one in Wichita who's never been caught. In it, he describes the kick he's getting as he slowly strangles the eleven-year-old daughter of a family he's just massacred. He's saying, 'There's no way I'm going to stop. There's only one way. You've got to lock me up—or death.'

"Well," Brooks continues, "that's it, except of course for old age. That'll put a stop to 'em, too. They get to a point where there's no way they can keep strangling the whores because the whores can whip 'em!"

As far as the northwest police know, or are willing to say, the Green River killings stopped in 1984. Assuming that the killer or killers have not been enfeebled by age, he or they could be dead, institutionalized or, as some West Coast police officials suspect, the murders are being committed in a new venue.

One often-mentioned possibility is San Diego.

There are several obvious, if superficial, reasons to suspect a link between the northwest killings and the San Diego cases. For one thing, the known Green River homicides stopped in 1984, just before the known San Diego killings began. This was perhaps a coincidence, too, but the dates strongly suggested continuity to many cops. Likewise, San Diego is a port town, just like Seattle. It has occurred to many investigators that the Green River cases might have been the work of itinerant navy personnel or merchant seamen who were stationed in the northwest and then transferred to southern California.

Such theories, while reasonable, do not account for important differences, however. One of the more telling contrasts, says Bob Keppel, was the crudeness of the earliest San Diego slayings. If "River Man," as he is sometimes known, had in fact relocated to San Diego, Keppel doubts that he'd forget the lessons he'd learned in Washington and Oregon. He would not, for instance, leave so many bodies to be found, the mark of an amateur, or of someone needing to call attention to his crimes. Keppel does not dispute that the Green River killer(s) may have moved on to hunt elsewhere, but he is inclined to think the new killing grounds are not around San Diego.

Five suspects have been arrested in connection with five prostitute murders in San Diego. However, none of those in custody can be connected to the remaining thirty-seven known or suspected homicides. Indeed, there never has been a single good suspect for the great majority of the slayings in San Diego.

In 1988, three local law enforcement agencies, the district attorney's office, the San Diego metropolitan police and the San Diego Sheriff's Department, banded together as the "San Diego Metropolitan Homicide Task Force" to jointly investigate the murders. This effort was criticized locally as too little done too late (the San Diego killings also appear to have stopped) to capture the mobile serial murderer. It has been a relatively low-key response—the task force's total budget has not exceeded $1 million—but the most telling criticism has been of the six-month deadline originally given its members to find their killer. "That's unrealistic," says Captain Evans in Seattle. "Unless you issue them crystal balls and magic wands, they can't do it."

Furthermore, the San Diego investigation has been hampered by the same problems that complicated the Green River case and every other instance of prostitute murder; few people are willing to come forward as witnesses (if they can remember anything) and others refuse to get involved, period. "We've had several parents who won't even admit that their daughters were hookers," says San Diego cop, "even though some of them have been arrested and convicted a dozen times. Do you think these parents will tell us all they know about [their daughters'] associates? Do you think the pimps are going to come forth and describe anybody?"

In the end, the Green River and San Diego investigations may not share a common suspect, or suspects, but they are otherwise alike in many other important ways. Enormous sums have been spent. Hundreds of thousands of man-hours of detective work have been put in. No one has been caught, and in all likelihood, no one will unless they make a mistake.

Still, experts such as Bob Keppel defend the task-force concept, if correctly implemented, as a perhaps wearying but nevertheless logical way to hunt the human hunters. It was a task force that cornered killer Wayne Williams in Atlanta. And it was a task force–type procedure, sifting through tens of thousands of parking tickets, that first enabled the New York City Police Department to place David Berkowitz in the vicinity of one of his "Son of Sam" shootings.

So, say the now severely curtailed teams of detectives in Seattle and San Diego, their task-force investigations will soldier on in search for the killers of at least ninety women. "After all," observes Keppel, "they can't just quit."

Readers with information that could lead to the identification and apprehension of the Green

River Killer are encouraged to contact the Green River Task Force: (206) 296-7575. Similarly, those with information concerning the possible identity of the San Diego Killer should contact the San Diego police homicide unit: (619) 531-2293.